ACTION RESEARCH IN THE SECONDARY SCHOOL: The Psychologist as Change Agent

Action research has become an important part of the movement for effectiveness and self-evaluation in schools. This book describes the interaction between an external change agent and heads and teachers in the secondary school on a number of projects including the creation of a social disadvantage index, remedial problems, attendance and truancy, parental involvement and parents evenings, home visits, school organisation and the evaluation of small-scale innovations.

It provides valuable guidelines for creating and administering action research projects in schools and there is a strong argument for more interaction between change agents, whether educational psychologists or university lecturers, and schools.

The book will be of use to all teachers and heads of schools involved in action research and to support service teachers, educational psychologists and local education authority advisers and inspectors.

R. Paul Gregory is Educational Psychologist at the City of Birmingham Education Department

ACTION RESEARCH IN THE SECONDARY SCHOOL

The Psychologist as Change Agent

R. PAUL GREGORY

with

J. Allebon
N.M. Gregory
C. Hackney
P. Meredith
A. Woodward

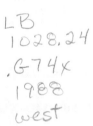

ROUTLEDGE
London and New York

First published in 1988 by
Routledge
a division of Routledge, Chapman and Hall
11 New Fetter Lane, London EC4P 4EE

Published in the USA by
Routledge
a division of Routledge, Chapman and Hall, Inc.
29 West 35th Street, New York NY 10001

Printed in Great Britain by Billing & Sons Ltd, Worcester

British Library Cataloguing in Publication Data

Gregory, R. Paul
    Action research in the secondary school:
    the psychologist as change agent.
    1. Secondary schools. Action research
    I. Title
    373.11'02'072
    ISBN 0-415-00122-6

Library of Congress Cataloging-in-Publication Data

ISBN 0-415-00122-6

CONTENTS

Contents

We trained hard, but it seemed that every time we were beginning to form up into teams we would be re-organised. I was to learn later in life that we tend to meet any new situation by re-organising: and a wonderful method it can be for creating the illusion of progress, while producing confusion, inefficiency and demoralization.

Roman centurion
Petronius Arbiter 210 BC

PREFACE

The work described in this book involves ten previously published papers about my work as an educational psychologist whilst acting in the role of external change-agent to largely one secondary school.

The chapters describe plans and activities carried out in an attempt to solve or ameliorate problems in this particular school. This action-research was undertaken in conjunction with the head teacher, deputy head, head of remedial department of the school and the area and school education welfare officers. The authors didn't just talk about action-research, or write about action-research, they did it.

This book is intended for other would-be external change-agents, for instance, local education authority (LEA) advisers, inspectors, LEA support service teachers, educational psychologists, lecturers in college and university departments of education and for head teachers, senior teachers, heads of departments, teachers and students who might like to work in partnership on action-research projects with any of the above change-agents, or on their own within their schools.

There is an accumulating literature about school effectiveness, school self-evaluation, teacher self-evaluation, educational innovation, school organisation development, use of internal and external change-agents, curriculum development, the teacher-as-researcher movement and action-research, voicing the growing need for all schools to critically examine their practices with a view to improvement. This book would have been worthwhile if only a few readers go on to participate in action-research projects in their schools with enthusiasm and optimism.

FOREWORD

Andrew Sutton

By the end of the last decade educational psychologists working in local authorities had begun a major shift in the nature of their practice. Critiques, analyses and prescriptions began to appear (in itself a major departure for a newly emerged semi-profession not previously troubled by self-doubt), the sometimes conflicting tendencies for reform being subsumed under the general rubric of 'reconstruction' (Gillham, 1979; McPherson and Sutton, 1981).

The varied outpourings of ink, then and subsequently, probably had little direct effect upon local-authority practice. Nevertheless, change there most certainly has been as a result of wider social movements and the practice of educational psychology in the late eighties is very different from that carried out under the same designation in the late seventies.

Present-day practice remains heterogeneous but definite trends are now clear in the redefinition of local-authority educational psychology over the last ten years or so. Foremost amongst these, most educational psychologists would surely agree, has been the radically changed status of psychometrics (mental measurement), once the mainstay of the claim to a scientific knowledge base. Educational psychologists have tried to distance themselves from the now disparaged role of 'tester', offering themselves instead as modifiers of how children act or learn, behaviourists rather than psychometrists (not such a great paradigm shift, some might say!). Secondly, from this has come a mushrooming of acronymous techniques and programmes, generally unvalidated, for modifying this or that behaviour, often directed towards groups of children rather than individuals and often extending beyond those who are taught to those who teach them. In the current wave of enthusiasm for locally based in-service teacher-training educational psychologists have therefore felt well placed to state their own potential contribution. Thirdly, there has been much talk (but no validated practice) about what educational psychologists could contribute 'at a systems level'.

What these trends have in common is an emphasis upon the educational rather than the psychological. The 'reconstruction' was never an articulated programme and the changes that have come about have been the outcome of wider forces. The practice of educational psychology appears to have been drawn by these forces into an encroachment on the fields of pedagogy and the roles of school manager and advisor. This encroachment is not generally welcome and its products have reopened the old, familiar accusation of psychological reductionism. It has also fitted in easily with a further powerful trend, common to all local-government semi-professions, towards a bureaucratisation of activities and a formalisation of professional relationships.

But educational psychology is no monolith. Individual psychologists have ploughed their own furrows, obviously affected by practical and organisational changes but determined, nevertheless, to pursue their personal reconstructions. Paul Gregory is one such psychologist. He became an educational psychologist in 1973, at the time of the first tentative questioning. His own personal response has been to hold on to the psychological and bring this to bear on the real-life problems met in his everyday practice. This has involved the use of mathematical analysis of data and the routine submission of his results to wider scrutiny through the pages of the technical literature. This book represents a part-record of his work.

It also represents a unique social record of the work of one psychologist in one school.

At the end of the eighties everything is coming round for further re-appraisal. School managers are going to look very carefully at where they direct their limited resources. When they want advice on how to organise the curriculum for less successful pupils or arrange to improve behaviour, should they look to the educational and management skills of their own senior and experienced staff or call in educational psychologists from outside? If they do call in outside consultants to help them, what sort of auxiliary help will they require? Perhaps the model of educational psychologist as psychologist is one that they might wish seriously to explore, as offering a service that supplements rather than encroaches upon their own roles as educationalists. Paul Gregory's work provides a chance to see what might be done.

Andrew Sutton
Director, Foundation for Conductive Education,
Birmingham

REFERENCES

Gillham, B. (1979) (ed.) Reconstructing Educational
    Psychology. London: Croom Helm
McPherson, I. and Sutton, A. (1981) (eds) Reconstructing
    Psychological Practice. London: Croom Helm

INTRODUCTION

Much educational research is being published that is relevant to the effectiveness of schools and teachers. However, its effect will be very limited unless practising teachers actually adopt and evaluate these new ideas for practice.

Even though there may be research evidence in the literature supporting the effectiveness of an innovation, only its successful implementation in a particular school will provide the much needed evidence of its local effect.

This point raises two interrelated questions:

(a) What are the best ways of successfully implementing an innovation in a school? and

(b) What evidence is there for the effectiveness of an innovation being carried out in a particular school?

These two issues are interrelated because one cannot have (b) without (a).

Many groups and individuals in teaching and allied professions endeavour to persuade others to take up new ideas. New head teachers try to do it with their staff; heads of departments in schools with those under them; local education authority (LEA) advisers and educational psychologists with schools and higher education courses with student teachers. It is assumed that those who promulgate these ideas have evidence to support them. (Maybe this is too charitable a view.) Not all such innovative ideas turn out to be as effective as first envisaged when applied in a particular school. It may have been problems with implementation that were the cause of the lack of effect (not necessarily the innovation per se); or else it may have been something lacking in the innovative idea itself. For these reasons it's important that innovations are piloted and evaluated on a small scale in a school before being extended on a larger scale.

This process of renewal or innovation is very problematic in all organisations and institutions but some writers consider it is especially so in education (Morrish, 1976). Nevertheless, it is one of the most important topics, not only within education, but society - if improvements in practice are to come about. It is therefore proper that this process be as well understood as possible not least because many innovations fail, wasting time and causing unnecessary upset and stress to those involved. According to Adams and Chen (1981), 70 per cent of all educational innovations supported by national governments, fail to achieve their original objectives. They may go on to achieve some but certainly not their prime ones.

Often one sees the published results of educational innovations or action-research in schools, namely relating to issue (b) but not an account of the hidden 'behind the scenes' events that hindered or promoted the progress of the research project; namely relating to issue (a). Adams and Chen (1981) report that rarely does this process, through which an innovation progresses from inception to complete implementation get described in detail.

Consequently, having recently achieved publication of the tenth paper in a series of papers describing innovation and action-research projects carried out largely with one comprehensive school between the years 1977 and 1984, it was considered apposite to publish these papers as a book, along with a description of the events that shaped the research across those seven years; the process of the innovation. This could only be done from detailed notes made at the time of these events.

For educational psychologists working in local education authorities, their greatest strength is also their greatest weakness; i.e. working in an applied setting, constantly being reminded of many of the real problems of children and teachers in the education system, but at the same time rarely having the time to carry out thorough long-term action-research with schools.

The Summerfield Report about the work of educational psychologists recommended that:

> Opportunities should be extended to some educational psychologists to undertake work in educational research and development, and to contribute to the understanding of human behaviour of other professions. (DES, 1968, p.xi)

Psychologists are not the only professionals who can take on this role of external change-agent with schools; LEA advisers, LEA support service teachers, college and university education department lecturers and publishers' representatives often assume the role. Some teachers have been trained to act in the capacity of internal change-agents within their own schools (Davie, 1980 and Davie et al., 1985).

There is considerable overlap in the definition of innovation and action-research and differences of emphasis between authors. Educational innovation is the deliberate attempt to improve educational practice (Munro, 1977) in relation to certain desired objectives (Dalin, 1973) and is different from 'change' which tends to be spontaneous and less planned and deliberate than innovation (Miles, 1964 and Morrish, 1976).

For action-research, Halsey (1972) described it as 'small scale intervention in the functioning of the real world and the close examination of the effects of such intervention'. Town (1973) saw affinities between action-research, curriculum development, the social experiment, evaluation research and programmes of systematic social action designed to promote change.

> Action research can be described as a process whereby in a given problem area, research is undertaken to specify the dimensions of the problem in its particular context; on the basis of this evidence a possible solution is formulated and is translated into action with a view to solving the problem; research is then used to evaluate the effectiveness of the action taken. (Town, 1973)

Powley and Evans (1979) also describe action-research as a means of evaluating social policy and in their work sought to bring about an integration between action and research as a workable whole.

A very different definition of action-research is given by Elliott (1978).

Basically classroom action-research relates to any teacher who is concerned with his own teaching; the teacher who is prepared to question his own approaches in order to improve its quality. Therefore the teacher is looking at what is actually going on in the classroom. He seeks to improve his own understanding of a particular problem rather than impose an instant solution upon that problem. Having collected information, it is crucial that time is taken for thought and reflection, although it is implicit in the idea of action-research that there should be some practical effect or end-product to the research: but based on an increased awareness of what actually happens in classrooms.

This represents the model used by the 'teacher as researcher movement' which according to Elliott (1981) can be traced to Lawrence Stenhouse and the Schools' Council's Humanities Curriculum Project which began in 1967. Gradually, accounts of teacher-based research are being written up, shared and made accessible (Nixon, 1981).

The orientation taken in this book is in sympathy with the teacher-as-researcher movement but owes its origins more to the definitions of Halsey (1972), Town (1973) and Powley and Evans (1979). It can be seen that 'action-research' is a subset of 'innovation'; it being the broader term. Depending upon whether an innovation is introduced by someone on the inside or the outside of the target institution, and at what levels, be it at grass roots or at top management level, there are different types of innovation.

Here, only grass root innovation will be described, but there are differences within this type. For example, 'Using a social disadvantage index' Chapter 1, 'Examining a secondary school's withdrawal system' Chapter 2, 'Attendance, social disadvantage, remedial reading and school organisation' Chapter 3 and 'The effectiveness of home visits by an EWO' Chapter 10 are all of the data-feedback and group problem-solving model (Kelman and Wolff, 1976). Here, data about the school were collected and the findings fed back to the staff of the school. This happened to varying degrees in these projects.

'Truancy: a plan for school-based action research' Chapter 4 was a planning paper whereas 'Parents' evenings in comprehensive schools: what are they for'? Chapter 5 was the prelude, or an introduction to a group-problem solving session by the school staff. 'Parental involvement in secondary school' Chapter 6 and 'Disadvantaged parents and contact with secondary school' Chapter 7 were an evaluation of the new-style parents' evening. Taken together the last three papers could equally be called action-research or problem-solving oriented innovation (Arends and Arends, 1977), as could 'Examining a secondary school's withdrawal system' Chapter 2, 'Corrective Reading programme: an evaluation' Chapters 8 and 9, if taken together. The chapters that follow are, except for the first, based on work carried out with one mixed comprehensive school - referred to as the study school.

REFERENCES

Adams, R.S. and Chen, D. (1981) The Process of Educational Innovation: An international perspective. London: Kogan Page and Paris: The UNESCO Press

Arends, R.I. and Arends, J.I. (1977) System Change Strategies in Educational Settings. London: Human Science Press

Dalin, P. (1973) Case Studies of Educational Innovation IV: Strategies for innovation in education. Centre for Educational Research and Innovation (CERI). Paris: Organisation for Economic Cooperation and Development (OECD)

Davie, R. (1980) 'In-service training directed at potential change-agents within school.' In R. Stratford (ed), The Child in Context. Applied Psychology for Children in the 1980s. Proceedings of the Division of Educational and Child Psychology, Annual Course. University of Southampton 1980. Leicester: British Psychological Society, Division of Educational and Child Psychology

Davie, R., Phillips, D. and Callely, E. (1985) Change in Secondary Schools. Cardiff: Department of Education, University of Cardiff, Welsh Office

D.E.S. (1968) Psychologists in Education Services (The Summerfield Report). London: HMSO

Elliott, J. (1978) 'Action-Research in Schools - some guidelines.' Paper presented at a conference at Girton College, Cambridge 7-9 July. Cambridge Institute of Education

Elliott, J. (1981) 'Forward'. In J. Nixon 1981. A Teacher's Guide to Action Research. London: Grant McIntyre

Halsey, A. (1972) 'E.P.A. action-research.' In Educational
   Priority Vol. 1: EPA Problems and Policies. London:
   HMSO
Kelman, E. and Wolff, G. (1976) 'Data feedback and group
   problem-solving: An   approach   to   organisational
   development in schools.' Psychology in Schools, 13, 4,
   421-7
Miles, M.B. (1964) Innovation in Education. New York:
   Teachers' College Press, Columbia University
Morrish, I. (1976) Aspects of Educational Change. London:
   George Allen and Unwin
Munro, R.G. (1977) Innovation: Success or Failure. London:
   Hodder and Stoughton
Nixon, J. (1981) A Teacher's Guide to Action-Research.
   London: Grant McIntyre
Powley, T. and Evans, D. (1979) 'Towards a methodology of
   action-research.' Journal of Social Policy, 8, 1, 27-46
Town, S.W. (1973) 'Action-research and social policy: some
   recent British experience.' Sociological Review, 21,
   573-98

To Susan

Chapter One

USING A SOCIAL DISADVANTAGE INDEX IN A SECONDARY SCHOOL*

The intention of this research was three-fold. Firstly, to test the feasibility of using a social disadvantage index within a secondary school, secondly to help the school identify at-risk children before they become a major problem in the hope that positive intervention via the pastoral care system might reduce the likelihood of future difficulties, and thirdly to test the possibility of using such an index to provide a parameter on which schools could be compared with others and over time with themselves (to note change in population within the school).

There are numerous ways one can attempt to select educationally at risk children (Wedell et al., 1976). Some of these methods are time consuming and costly in manpower.
What is required is a technique which would provide as much predictive information about the child for least expense using data that are easily available within schools.
A social disadvantage index appears to provide this, in that such children identified are known to be at much greater risk than the general population of going into local authority care failing educationally and becoming delinquent.
One should be aware that there are a number of predictors or sets of predictors of delinquency and these appear to overlap with indices of social disadvantage.

* Reproduced from Remedial Education, 14, 1, 5-11, 1979 by kind permission of the National Association for Remedial Education.

1

PREDICTORS OF DELINQUENCY

(a) Having delinquent older siblings. (Phillips et al., (1972) found that this alone predicted 93 per cent of the delinquents in his sample.)
(b) Having low motivation for school.
(c) Being below average verbal ability.
(d) Being below average reading ability.

Taking a, b, c and d together gave 100 per cent prediction of delinquents in Phillips et al. (1972) study of disadvantaged families.

West and Farrington (1977) found that having three or more of the following factors gave an 80 per cent prediction of a child getting a criminal record.

1. The child has any member of his family (including parents) with a criminal record.
2. The child comes from a family with low income.
3. The child is one of a large family (four or more children).
4. The child has low ability (less than the 25th percentile or IQ 90).
5. The child has suffered unsatisfactory parental upbringing (as judged by a social worker).

West and Farrington (1977) found that many delinquents do stop their criminal activity but that a particular group do not. Factors relating to boys who continue their delinquency after the age of 19 were:

1. Criminality in any member of the child's family.
2. The family having low income.
3. The family having four or more children.
4. The child having a high score on West and Farrington's anti-social scale.

Intelligence and parental upbringing were not found to be relevant in predicting continued delinquency. If a young delinquent is outside of these four factors he is likely to be non-delinquent after the age of 19. West and Farrington (1977) suggest that most delinquents stop their criminality by the age of 23.

Davies (1976) in her study of girls aged 14 to 16 appearing before the courts, found a very similar picture.

The court girls (as compared to a control group) were less motivated for school, had parents who were seen as less co-operative with school, 75 per cent truanted (25 per cent of the controls did so). They had lower intelligence and were doing badly at school.

Ill health, poor housing and low income characterised their families. Eighty per cent of the girls had friends who had been to court. Davies distinguished between (a) those appearing in court for committing offences and (b) those in need of care protection or control.

Offenders tended to have difficulties in school work where as the behaviour of the others appeared to be a reaction to stress in the family.

About half of the court and control group girls had been helped by people in authority (teachers, social workers, etc.) and found them helpful. Despite this more than half the court girls felt that no one had helped them. The court girls felt that their problems were relationships with boyfriends and conflicts with their parents.

Social disadvantage is obviously a factor in Davies's sample of girls in trouble. It is noticeable that the index used by Wedge and Prosser (1973) of bad housing, low income, one-parent or large families is largely applicable.

For this present study the index described by Herbert (1976) seemed most appropriate. The factors used are such that the information could easily be collected in a school.

(a) Quality of child's clothing.
(b) School attendance.
(c) Parental occupation.
(d) Family size.
(e) Parents' contact with school.

A small alteration was made (Herbert, 1977) to allow the inclusion of one-parent families - another group known to be at risk of social disadvantage.

Not only might such indices as described above be used by schools but also by Social Services Observation and Assessment Centres (Cooper, 1975).

METHOD

The study was undertaken in a girls' secondary school which was previously selective but now has two years of comprehensive intake, in a largely working class urban area of Birmingham, consisting mainly of council housing, older multiple-occupied and some owner-occupied houses. The data were collected in March 1977.

The school has 4/5 form intake and has approximately 700 pupils. The sample consisted of all the pupils in the first year forms (N = 123). (They would be aged between 11 and 12.) The forms were organised such that class 1N (N = 32) and 1S (N = 32) were upper band, 1W (N = 24) and 1E (N = 24) were lower band and 1WH (N = 11) was a small remedial class. There was mixed ability within bands.

DATA

School reports, medical cards (12M) and teacher assessments were the source of the information.

INDEX

Each child was scored a number of points for each factor on which she qualified.

One-parent family (2 pts).
Very poor clothing (3 pts).
Attendance below 75 per cent with no reasonable excuse (3 pts); between 75-90 per cent with reasonable excuse (1 pt).
Father (or mother if a one-parent family) Social Class V unskilled or chronically unemployed (2 pts).
Father (or mother if a one-parent family) Social Class IV (semi-skilled) (1 pt).
Five or more children in the family (2 pts).
Three or four children in the family (1 pt).
Parents hardly ever seen in school except when asked in emergency (1 pt).

A total score between 5 and 13 points would indicate disadvantage. The attendance score was based on attendance between September and December 1976 (given on the school report). Children in the care of the local authority were automatically noted as disadvantaged.
Other data collected were:

(a)   Whether the child was on free dinners.

(b) Ethnic group.
(c) Motivation for school.
(d) Criminality in the family.
(e) Had the child any convictions.
(f) Reading ability less than reading age eight.

c, d and e were judged from the form teacher's knowledge. For motivation, the teacher was asked whether she rated the child's motivation for school (regardless of her work standard) as being low or adequate.

RESULTS

Below are given the characteristics of the total sample.

Two thirds of the sample children are from Social Class III or higher and one-third from Class IV and V.

The sample consists of nearly 75 per cent indigenous children with the largest minority group being black. Indigenous children are under represented in the remedial class where there is an over representation of Irish and Asian children. Black children appear to be evenly distributed between the two bands and certainly do not predominate in the lower forms.

As one would expect children from the largest families tend to be in the lower forms and particularly the remedial class whereas those from small families tend to be in the higher classes.

DISADVANTAGED CHILDREN

Table 1.4: Form-bands analysed by disadvantage

	Disadvantaged pupils	
Upper band		
1N and 1S N = 64	(N = 4)	6.3%
Lower band		
1E and 1W N = 48	(N = 7)	14.6%
Remedial		
1Wh N = 11	(N = 4)	36.3%
Total N = 123	(N = 15)	12.2%

Table 1.1: Socio-economic status

	Class III (or higher)	Class IV	Class V	Unknown
Upper band 1N and 1S N = 64	(N = 55) 86%	(N = 5) 7.8%	(N = 3) 4.6%	(N = 1) 1.6%
Lower band 1E and 1W N = 48	(N = 20) 41%	(N = 8) 16.8%	(N = 6) 12.8%	(N = 14) 29.4%
Remedial 1Wh N = 11	(N = 7) 63%	(N = 1) 9%	(N = 2) 18.4%	(N = 1) 9.3%
Total 123	(N = 82) 66.7%	(N = 14) 11.4%	(N = 11) 8.9%	(N = 16) 13%

Table 1.2: Ethnic groups

The ethnic composition of the sample

	Black	Irish	Asian	Indigenous
Upper band 1N and 1S N = 64	(N = 10) 15.6%	(N = 1) 1.5%	(N = 0) 0%	(N = 53) 82.9%
Lower band 1E and 1W N = 48	(N = 9) 18.8%	(N = 4) 8.3%	(N = 2) 4.2%	(N = 33) 68.7%
Remedial 1Wh N = 11	(N = 3) 27.2%	(N = 1) 9.1%	(N = 2) 18.2%	(N = 5) 45.5%
Total	(N = 22) 17.9%	(N = 6) 4.8%	(N = 4) 3.3%	(N = 91) 74%

Table 1.3: Family size: Form bands analysed by family size

	5+ children	3-4 children	2 or less children
Upper band			
1N and 1S N = 64	(N = 7) 10.9%	(N = 18) 28.1%	(N = 39) 61%
Lower band			
1E and 1N N = 48	(N = 17) 35.4%	(N = 15) 31.3%	(N = 16) 33.3%
Remedial			
1Wh N = 11	(N = 7) 63.6%	(N = 3) 27.3%	(N = 1) 9.1%
Total N = 123	(N = 31) 25.2%	(N = 36) 29.3%	(N = 56) 45.5%

Of the first-year pupils 12.2 per cent are socially disadvantaged. Such pupils are predominant in the lower forms and constitute nearly 40 per cent of the remedial class. Herbert (1976) suggests that in a deprived area up to 30 per cent of a school population would probably be disadvantaged. Nationally for 11-year-old children, Wedge and Prosser (1973) found that 6 per cent were disadvantaged.

Table 1.5: Disadvantaged children and reading ability

	Disadvantaged N = 15	Not disadvantaged N = 108
Poor readers	(N = 4) 26%	(N = 7) 6.5%
Adequate readers	(N = 11) 74%	(N = 101) 93.5%

There are four times more poor readers in the disadvantaged group than in the control group. For the total sample 9 per cent are poor readers, i.e. reading age below eight years.

Table 1.6: Disadvantaged children and motivation for school

	Disadvantaged N = 15	Not disadvantaged N = 108
Low motivation	(N = 4) 26%	(N = 10) 9.3%
Adequate motivation	(N = 11) 74%	(N = 98) 90.7%

There are three times more children who have low motivation for school in the disadvantaged group than in the controls. Over the whole sample, 11.4 per cent were felt by teachers to have low motivation.

Table 1.7: Ethnic groups

	Black children and disadvantage	
	Disadvantaged N = 15	Not disadvantaged N = 108
Black	(N = 3) 20%	(N = 19) 17.6%
Not black	(N = 12) 80%	(N = 89) 82.4%

Black children are no more likely to be disadvantaged than

the control group.

Table 1.8: Irish children and disadvantage

	Disadvantaged N = 15	Not disadvantaged N = 108
Irish	(N = 3) 20%	(N = 3) 2.8%
Not Irish	(N = 12) 80%	(N = 105) 97.2%

There are nearly seven times more children of Irish origin in the disadvantaged group than in the control group.

Table 1.9: Asian children and disadvantage

	Disadvantaged N = 15	Not disadvantaged N = 108
Asian	(N = 1) 6.6%	(N = 3) 2.7%
Not Asian	(N = 14) 93.4%	(N = 105) 97.3%

Twice as many Asian children fall into the disadvantaged group compared to the control group. No children were known to have convictions for delinquency or to be from criminal families.

CONCLUSION

Disadvantaged children constitute approximately 12 per cent of the sample and these children are more likely to be poorly motivated for school, poor readers and of Irish or Asian origin (but not black). When compared to the control group (i.e. all the children not disadvantaged N = 108).

Only one child was disadvantaged, poorly motivated for school and a poor reader and she was in the care of the local authority. She should be seen as particularly at risk.

Other categories of children

It is of interest now to see how other groups of children fare in school and in particular those from one-parent families. Since this was a factor in the disadvantage index some of the hypotheses about this group will be obvious.

Table 1.10: Children living in one-parent families

Upper band 1N and 1S N = 64	N = 6	9.4%
Lower band 1E and 1W N = 48	N = 9	18.8%
Remedial 1Wh N = 11	N = 2	18%
Total N = 123	N = 17	13.8%

There are twice as many children of one-parent families in the lower band and remedial class than in the upper band and approximately 14 per cent of the children in the first year live with one parent.

Forty-three children or 35 per cent live with one parent or a large family (five or more children).

This is much higher than Wedge and Prosser (1973) found in a national sample of 10,000 11-year-old children in which 23 per cent of children had one parent or lived in a large family.

Table 1.11: One-parent families and disadvantage

	One-parent family N = 17	Two-parent family N = 106
Disadvantaged	(N = 7) 41%	(N = 8) 7.5%
Not disadvantaged	(N = 10) 59%	(N = 98) 92.5%

Children from one-parent families are more than five times more likely to be disadvantaged when compared to children from two-parent families.

School non-attendance

Table 1.12 shows that 26 per cent of these pupils attend school for 90 per cent of time or less, and of the total pupils only 9.8 per cent are losing time without reasonable excuse.

There are more than twice as many pupils with lower attendance in the lower band compared to the upper band. Attendance in the remedial class is similar to that for the total sample.

10

Table 1.12: The attendance level of the sample

Level of attendance		Number of children with a reasonable excuse	Number of children with no reasonable excuse
90% or more	(N = 91) 74%		
75-90%	(N = 24) 19.5%	(N = 18) 14.6%	(N = 6) 4.9%
Less than 75%	(N = 8) 6.5%	(N = 2) 1.6%	(N = 6) 4.9%
Total	N = 123	(N = 20) 16.2%	(N = 12) 9.8%

Table 1.13: Distribution of school non-attendance

	Pupils attending less than 90%	With excuse	Without excuse
Upper band			
1N and 1S N = 64	(N = 11) 17.1%	(N = 7) 10.9%	(N = 4) 6.2%
Lower band			
1E and 1W N = 48	(N = 18) 37.5%	(N = 11) 23%	(N = 7) 14.5%
Remedial			
1Wh N = 11	(N = 3) 27%	(N = 2) 18%	(N = 1) 9%
Total N = 123	(N = 32) 26%	(N = 20) 16.2%	(N = 12) 9.8%

Pupils with less than 90 per cent attendance without reasonable excuse are taken as poor attenders (N = 12). And one finds that 58 per cent of these children are disadvantaged compared to 7.2 per cent for good attenders thus poor attenders are eight times more likely to be disadvantaged.

Such findings are consistent with those of Fogelman and Richardson's (1974) and Sutton (1975).

Table 1.14: Attendance compared to disadvantage

	Poor attenders N = 12		Good attenders N = 111	
Disadvantaged	(N =	7) 58%	(N =	8) 7.2%
Not disadvantaged	(N =	5) 42%	(N =	103) 92.8%

Table 1.15: Attendance compared to reading ability

	Poor readers N = 11		Good readers N = 112	
Poor attenders	(N =	1) 10%	(N =	11) 11%
Good attenders	(N =	10) 90%	(N =	101) 89%

Table 1.15 indicates that in this school being a poor reader is not associated with being a poor attender, i.e. 10 per cent of poor readers are poor attenders and a similar proportion of good readers are likewise.

Table 1.16: Attendance compared to poor motivation

	Poor attenders N = 12		Good attenders N = 111	
Poor motivation	(N =	3) 25%	(N =	11) 10%
Adequate motivation	(N =	9) 75%	(N =	100) 90%

Poor attenders are two-and-a-half times more likely to be poorly motivated than good attenders.

Poorly motivated children

Table 1.17: A comparison of poorly motivated children with ethnic group

Ethnic group	Poor motivation N = 14		Adequate motivation N = 109	
Black	(N = 5)	35.7%	(N = 17)	15.5%
Irish	(N = 1)	7.1%	(N = 5)	4.5%
Asian	(N = 0)	0%	(N = 4)	3.7%
Indigenous	(N = 8)	57.2%	(N = 83)	76.1%

This table shows that there are more than twice as many black girls in the poorly motivated group than in the control group. This seems surprising since of the minority groups the black children appear to be doing best in this school and such children are not particularly socially disadvantaged.

Table 1.18: Comparison of motivation and reading ability

	Poor readers N = 11		Good readers N = 112	
Poor motivation	(N = 3)	27%	(N = 11)	10%
Adequate motivation	(N = 8)	73%	(N = 101)	90%

Poor readers are nearly three times more likely to be poorly motivated than good readers.

CONCLUSION

Using a disadvantage index in a secondary school has been a feasible operation and for the time it has cost, has yielded much information. It has identified a number of 'at risk' children but one is at pains to emphasise that it is hoped that such identification should lead to development of positive attitudes and intervention. This would include the child's pastoral care tutor or form teacher making a particular effort to develop a positive relationship with the child and his parents. The organisation within this school provides opportunities for formal contact with parents

(parents' evenings) and informal contact for new parents (a wine and cheese evening in the first term) and they appear to be readily welcomed when they visit the school. The size of classes decreases towards the lower band and remedial forms and this must again favour the more disadvantaged pupils.

The data generated by this study is now available to compare with other schools and positive suggestions for solution of problems may be a pay-off.

The results indicate that this school has twice the national average of socially disadvantaged pupils but not as high as one would expect in a 'deprived' area. These pupils were found to be at greater risk of being poorly motivated, poor readers and to belong to minority groups (Irish or Asian but not black).

Seventy-four per cent of the pupils were attending at a rate of 90 per cent or more with approximately 10 per cent losing time without reasonable excuse. Non-attendance seems to be a greater problem in the lower band, and poor attending children without reasonable excuses tend to be disadvantaged, poorly motivated but not poor readers in this school. This suggests that the way this school caters for poor readers may help them avoid being non-attenders.

Black girls are more likely than others to be seen as low in motivation for school even though they tend not to be disadvantaged and are performing better than the other minority groups. However, poor readers are nearly three times more likely to be poorly motivated for school compared to adequate readers (but again, poor readers are more likely to be disadvantaged!).

REFERENCES

Cooper, R. (1975) Social Services Department's Observation and Assessment Centres for Children M.O.P.P. Discussion paper 3 Movement of Practising Psychologists

Davies, I. (1976) 'Girls appearing before a juvenile Court' Further Studies of Female Offenders. Home Office Research Study No 33. H.M.S.O.

Fogelman, K. and Richardson, K. (1974) 'School attendance. Some results from the National Child Development Study', B. Turner (ed.) Truancy. London: Ward Lock Educational

Herbert, G.W. (1976) 'Social problems: identification and action' The Early Identification of Educationally 'at risk' Children Wedell, K. and Raybould, E.C. (eds) Educational Review Occasional Paper No 6. University of Birmingham

Herbert, G.W. (1977) (Personal communication.)

Phillips, C.J. et al. (1972) 'Child Development Study'. School of Education. University of Birmingham

Sutton, A. (1975) 'Children on interim care orders for non-attendance at school. An essay in the use of individual case studies as a means of surveying current practice and needs'. Parent and Child Centre, Birmingham

Wedge, P. and Prosser, H. (1973) Born to Fail. National Children's Bureau. London: Arrow Books

West, D.I. and Farrington, D.P. (1977) The Delinquent Way of Life. Cambridge studies in Criminology. London: Heinemann

Wedell, K. et al. (1976) The Early Identification of Educationally 'at risk' Children (op. cit.)

Chapter Two

EXAMINING A SECONDARY SCHOOL'S WITHDRAWAL
SYSTEM OF HELP FOR PUPILS WITH REMEDIAL
PROBLEMS. AN EXAMPLE OF WITHIN-SCHOOL
EVALUATION*

INTRODUCTION

The work of educational psychologists in school
psychological and child guidance services has largely been
restricted to dealing with individual referrals of children
presenting as a problem. A survey of the practice of
psychologists in problems of school attendance (Sutton,
1975) revealed that some psychologists seemed wholly
unaware of the fact that the behaviour of institutions and
professions as much as that of the client involved, merited
psychological investigation. The survey asked about current
and future projections of practice with individual referral of
non-attending children and the relationship between
psychological services and education welfare services. In the
replies there was no mention of the psychologists' potential
role in investigating the contribution of factors in individual
schools to the generation of attendance problems.

The following study is possibly a small step towards the
development of such a role for psychologists. The intention
was to examine the connection between social disadvantage,
poor attendance, poor reading and school organisation. It is
well known that children from socially disadvantaged homes
are at greater risk than the general population of going into
local authority care, failing educationally and becoming
delinquent. The question is, how do disadvantaged children
fare in particular secondary schools? It may be that some
schools by the way they are organised play a part in actively

*Reprinted by kind permission from the Journal of Applied
Educational Studies, 12, 1, 44-55, 1983

reducing the risk of educational failure with these children.

PROCEDURE

This study was undertaken in one mixed comprehensive school (with two years of comprehensive intake - being previously a secondary-modern school). The school is situated in the West Midlands and draws its pupils from mainly a single council housing estate, and a few owner-occupied houses. The data was collected in June 1977.

The school had a four-class intake and approximately 600 pupils. The sample consisted of all the pupils in the first-year forms (N = 101, 63 boys, 38 girls). They were aged between eleven and twelve. The pupils were organised into four mixed ability classes, with children being withdrawn into groups of five or six for remedial English, Maths and Handwriting. Apparently the work was set by the remedial teacher but was supervised by whichever teacher was free at the time.

Generally the intake of pupils was felt by the school to be largely of low reading ability. Data was derived from the attendance register, medical cards, personal files and scores of reading tests (Schonell A) administered by the remedial teacher.

The social disadvantage index was used in which each child was scored a number of points for each factor on which he qualified. This index was as follows:

One-parent family	Score 2	points
Having very poor clothing	3	
Having attendance below 75% (with no reasonable excuse)	3	
Having attendance between 75-90% (with no reasonable excuse)	1	
Father (or mother if a one-parent family) unskilled or chronically unemployed (Social Class V)	2	
Father (or mother if a one-parent family) is semi-skilled (Social Class IV)	1	
5 or more children in family	2	
3 or 4 children in family	1	

17

If parents were hardly ever   1
seen in school except in an
emergency

   A total of between 5 and 13 points would indicate social
disadvantage. The attendance score was based on the
attendance for the first term at school. Children identified
by this index could become the focus of pastoral care, since
they are the ones mostly like to fail in school. A school
could easily do this themselves.
   The social disadvantage index will not be described in
further detail here. (For this see Herbert, 1976, Gregory,
1979).
   Other data collected were

(a) whether the child was withdrawn or not for extra help.
     Pupils were withdrawn for extra English or for all three
     subjects, English, Maths and Handwriting. Those in this
     latter group were withdrawn for most lessons.
(b) Motivation for school - teachers were asked to rate all
     pupils as adequate or low in motivation for school
     regardless of the standard of their work.

RESULTS

Table 2.1: Percentage of pupils' families and their socio-
economic status

	Social Class III or higher	Class IV	Class V	Unknown
Total sample	40	29	20	11

   Table 2.1 indicates that just over one-third of the first-
year intake of this school were of social class III or higher.
91% of the pupils were from the white indigenous
population. Wedge and Prosser 1973 found that 23% of a
national sample of 10,000 eleven-year-old children came
from one-parent or large families (having five or more
children). In this sample nearly 60% of pupils were in this
category.

Table 2.2: Percentage of pupils and their reading ages (N = 93)

Pupils at or above their   27
chronological age in reading (i.e. age 11)

Pupils below their chronological age   73
in reading

More than two-thirds of the sample was below average in reading ability. In fact 27% had reading ages of eight or less on entry to the school.

Social disadvantage

21% of the pupils were found to live in socially disadvantaged homes. Herbert 1976 suggests that in a deprived area up to 30% of a school population would probably be disadvantaged. These figures can be compared to Wedge and Prosser's (1973) finding that 6% of eleven-year-old children nationally were disadvantaged.

Table 2.3: Withdrawn pupils and socially disadvantaged

	Percentage of pupils socially disadvantaged
Withdrawn for English N = 24	33
Withdrawn for English Maths and Handwriting N = 12	25
Total Sample (N = 101)	21

Table 2.3 indicates that there was a tendency for socially disadvantaged pupils to be withdrawn for extra help.

Table 2.4: Disadvantaged children and reading ability

	Disadvantaged N = 21	Not disadvantaged N = 80
Poor readers	(N = 9) 43%	(N = 16) 20%
Adequate readers	(N = 12) 57%	(N = 64) 80%

19

Poor readers were defined as being at or below a reading age of eight years. Nearly half of the disadvantaged pupils were poor readers and they were twice as likely to be in this category than non-disadvantaged pupils (control).

Table 2.5: Disadvantaged children and motivation for school

	Disadvantaged N = 21	Not disadvantaged N = 80
Low motivation	(N = 4) 19%	(N = 6) 8%
Adequate motivation	(N = 17) 81%	(N = 74) 92%

Disadvantaged pupils are more than twice as likely than the controls to be of low motivation for school, judging from the teachers' perception. They are also likely to be poor readers and consequently being withdrawn for extra help.

It would appear that this school being unable to give extra help to every pupil has in fact selected a high number of socially disadvantaged pupils for this facility.

These would be just the children which are found to be at risk educationally. The next question is, does this special help have a positive effect? A partial answer to this was explored through comparison of attendance records over the year. However other questions not addressed here might be: do the withdrawn pupils show better motivation for school and improved reading ability?

School attendance

Table 2.6 indicates that 67% of the first-year pupils of this school attend for more than 90% of the time. However, this figure falls for the following terms.

Pupils attending for less than 75% of the time increases from 11 to 17% by the third term. Non-attendance is an increasing problem across the three terms - and remember that these are children new to a comprehensive school and all that it has to offer. If so many pupils are beginning to reduce their attendance so early in their secondary school career, we must ask whether this trend continues in the second and subsequent years in the school. No data is provided to answer this but the education welfare officer serving the school finds most of his clients coming from the

Table 2.6: Attendance level of sample compared for three terms (September 1976 – July 1977)

Attendance	1st Term			2nd Term			3rd Term		
	Total %	Boys %	Girls %	Total %	Boys %	Girls %	Total %	Boys %	Girls %
More than 90%	67	60	76	53	56	50	55	57	51
Between 75-90%	22	29	13	29	32	24	28	32	22
Less than 75%	11	11	11	18	12	26	17	11	27

Table 2.7: Percentage of poor-attending pupils, comparing those withdrawn with the total sample for three terms

| | Pupils attending for less than 90% of the time | | | | | | | | |
| | Term 1 | | | Term 2 | | | Term 3 | | |
	Total	Boys	Girls	Total	Boys	Girls	Total	Boys	Girls
Withdrawn for English (N = 24)	46	44	50	54	50	67	58	56	67
Withdrawn for English, Maths and Handwriting	42	38	50	58	50	75	75	75	75
Total Sample (N = 101)	34	40	24	47	44	50	45	43	49

third, fourth and particularly the fifth-year pupils. This would suggest the trend of non-attendance does continue. Do all secondary schools show this trend? Whatever the answer, this particular school needs to consider how the school organisation, curriculum and staff behaviour might be influencing attendance.

The attendance of the girls can be seen from Table 2.6 to be a particular problem: namely 27% of girls are attending for less than 75% of the time by the third term. This is consistent with the findings of Bransby 1951 and West Riding 1962 that secondary school girls generally attend less well than boys (see Table 2.7).

Table 2.7 shows the percentage of pupils who were attending for less than 90% of the time at school, comparing those withdrawn for extra help, with the total sample. The table shows that an increasing proportion of those withdrawn attend less well as the year progresses. This is particularly apparent for girls and for those who are withdrawn the most number of lessons. By the third term 75% of this group are attending for less than 90% of school time. Since the rate of disadvantage in this withdrawn group is 25% as compared to 21% for the total sample, the poor attendance can not be explained by saying that it has many more disadvantaged pupils (see table 2.3).

Table 2.8: A comparison of pupils withdrawn for English, Maths and Handwriting with pupils not withdrawn for Term 3

	Withdrawn (N = 12)	Not Withdrawn (N = 88)
Poor Attender	9	36
Good Attender	3	52

Chi square = 3.38 P < .02

Poor attenders were taken as those attending for 90% of the time or less.

It may be that remedial curriculum co-ordination needs examination. The assumption that withdrawing pupils from their main class lessons for extra help is beneficial to the pupil, may not be valid in this school. Further research would be necessary to see how far these findings might be generalised to other schools.

Disadvantaged pupils were found to be more likely than the controls to be poor attenders, less well motivated for school, poor readers and thus more likely to be withdrawn.

Since pupils withdrawn for extra help are associated with poor attendance it follows that poor readers are likely to be at risk of poor attendance in this school. This was not found to be the case in a girls' comprehensive school in the same neighbourhood as the study school. In the girls' school (Gregory, 1979) the comparable remedial pupils were attending as well as the average attendance for the whole of the first year. A difference was that at the girls' school remedial pupils were not withdrawn; they were in one small class with one teacher for a large proportion of their timetable. The classes were not organised into mixed ability but had an upper and middle band of two classes each and a remedial class. It may be that the way a school organises its pupils for teaching has an effect on pupil attendance.

CONCLUSION

Data available in the school, even though analysed in an uncomplicated manner, have provided enough evidence to make some hypotheses more tenable than others in respect of this school. It is hoped that this demonstrates how within-school evaluation might be profitable for a school to undertake either itself or with a psychologist.

The school that was the focus of this study has changed the way it organises the first-year pupils, to one upper and one middle ability class leaving two smaller parallel remedial classes. A group of first-year children with reading ages less than nine years on the Daniels and Diack Test 12 Test of Reading Experience (Daniels and Diack, 1972) were taught using a new American reading programme for secondary aged pupils, and compared to a control group of similar pupils using the school's current remedial equipment. The experimental group had one teacher, the control group received two. However this was an improvement over the situation cited earlier where the withdrawn pupils received any teacher who was free at the time resulting in the pupils seeing many different teachers. The results described by Gregory, Hackney and Gregory 1982 were very encouraging. The experimental group gained 1.8 years in reading in five months' teaching whilst the control group in the same time, gained 0.2 years. The experimental group also maintained good school behaviour and improved attendance more so than the control group.

Thus what started out as an exploratory study and within-school evaluation, led on to change of practice and further evaluation - showing that improved curriculum can result in improved attendance of children with reading problems. Evaluation should not be a one-off operation but an integral part of the activities of a school. School Psychological Service' psychologists could have a role in helping schools carry out within-school evaluation. They should more systematically attempt to find out what effect their practices have on pupils. It may be that the traditional practice of psychologists being involved with individual referrals has helped schools avoid examining their own behaviour with reference to children who present as a problem for them.

REFERENCES

Bransby, E. (1951) 'A study of absence from school.' Medical Officer 86 pp. 223-30

Daniels, J.C. and Diack, H. (1972) The Standard Reading Tests. London: Chatto and Windus

Gregory, R.P. (1979) 'Using a social disadvantage index in a Secondary School.' Remedial Education Vol. 14 No. 1 pp. 5-11

Gregory, R.P., Hackney, C. and Gregory, N.M. (1982) 'Corrective Reading Programme: An evaluation.' British Journal of Educational Psychology. 52 pp. 33-50

Herbert, G.W. (1976) 'Social problems: Identification and action.' Wedell, K. and Raybould, E.C. (eds) The Early Identification of Educationally 'at risk' children. Educational Review Occasional paper No. 6. University of Birmingham

Sutton, A. (1975) A Brief Survey of Educational Psychologists' Involvement with Problems of School Attendance Conducted in the West Midlands Area 1971. Parent and Child Centre A.H.A. Birmingham

Wedge, P. and Prosser, H. (1973) Born to Fail. National Children's Bureau. London: Arrow Books

West Riding County Council Education Committee (1962) 'Two enquiries into attendance in secondary schools.' Unpublished report

Chapter Three

ATTENDANCE, SOCIAL DISADVANTAGE, REMEDIAL
READING AND SCHOOL ORGANISATION: A COMPARISON
OF TWO NEIGHBOURING COMPREHENSIVE SCHOOLS*

INTRODUCTION

Comparing schools and drawing conclusions is fraught with
problems and pitfalls. However, there has been an increasing
interest in trying to define what is successful and what is
not in education. The D.E.S. recently published a pamphlet
entitled 'Ten Good Schools' in an attempt to open discussion
on this question. This pamphlet hopefully will be successful
in opening discussion but as a model for evaluation leaves
much to be desired. Ten schools were selected as being
successful and their outstanding features were drawn from
them. A control group of bad schools was not apparent and
thus it was not known whether these outstanding features
taken to be contributory to the success of a secondary
school were to be found in bad schools as well.

The rate of occurrence of behaviour problems in schools
has been found to vary between schools such that the
differences are not explained by the schools being in
different areas (Gath et al., 1972).

Galloway (1976) and Reynolds et al. (1974) found large
differences between schools in rates of absenteeism.
Reynolds found the differences remained consistent over a
period of six years. The size of school was of little
importance for school attendance rates - but absenteeism
was more frequent in schools taking a high proportion of
socially disadvantaged children as assessed by the proportion
on free school meals (Galloway, 1976).

* Reprinted by kind permission from the Journal of the
Association of Educational Psychologists, 5, 10, 56-60, 1982

Galloway also found that suspension rates in secondary schools in Sheffield were not uniform, but that former selective schools showed the highest rate. He concluded suspension rates may not reflect the amount or degree of deviant behaviour in the school.

In a longitudinal study of secondary school pupils in which their initial behaviour on entry to the school was taken into account, Yule and Rutter (1976) found that in some schools scarcely any children showed behaviour difficulties whereas in others nearly 50% did so. The authors attribute these differences to differences in the schools. They found that primary schools also varied greatly in the proportion of children with behaviour problems even after taking into account where the child lived and whether or not they came from a disturbed or socially disadvantaged home. Rates of disturbance were highest in schools with a high rate of staff and pupil turnover and a high proportion of children from immigrant families.

Thus children's behaviour may be shaped by the school to an important extent but according to Rutter and Madge (1976) little as yet is known about which factors in the school environment make for these differences or how they operate. (Rutter et al., 1979 makes a good initial contribution however.) This may be because relatively little finance has been put into educational research. More money is spent in medical research in one year than has been spent in the entire history of educational research (Tizard, 1974).

There are, however, many interesting suggestions on how school organisation impinges on pupils (Biddle, 1970) and how schools appear to have a distinctive atmosphere which sets the tone of expectations for staff and pupils (McDill, Myers and Rigsby, 1974). It would be fallacious to assume that one comprehensive school is much the same as another. LEA educational psychologists could easily fall into the misapprehension that the comprehensives they cover all had the same need for the same type of psychological service. The above evidence indicates that comprehensives can be very different in the type of child-intake and in the success with which they shape desirable behaviours in their pupils. The present study was exploratory and intended to discover and compare the school attendance rates, children with reading problems and the relative percentages of socially disadvantaged children in two neighbouring comprehensive schools. This was to be a preliminary examination of the similarities and differences that existed in the first-year intake to both schools, with a view to beginning an assessment of the schools' needs in regard to psychological service from their LEA psychologist. Tentative comparisions between school organisation were considered.

METHOD

The first-year intake for year 1976/77 was compared for two neighbouring comprehensive schools in Birmingham.

School A is an all girls school with 700 pupils and 4/5 form intake. It was previously selective and became comprehensive 7 years ago. It draws its intake from mainly council housing, older multiply occupied and some owner-occupied houses. The forms were organised into bands with two mixed ability classes in an upper band, two in a lower band and a small remedial class of approximately 11 pupils. The pupils were placed in the bands according to ability as judged from information received from the primary school. Those in the remedial class spent approximately half their timetable with one teacher (Gregory, 1979).

School B is a mixed school previously non-selective becoming comprehensive 7 years ago with 630 pupils and 4 form intake. Its intake comes largely from council housing with relatively few children from owner-occupied houses. The forms were organised on a mixed ability basis with children being randomly assigned. On top of this, a system of withdrawal operated in which children could be withdrawn for extra remedial work in English and/or Maths and/or Handwriting. The remedial work was set by the remedial teacher and supervised by whichever teacher was free at the time with groups of five to six children (Gregory, 1982).

DATA COLLECTION

123 children in school A and 101 children in school B aged between 11 and 12 years were involved in this study. Each child was rated for his social disadvantage using an index, (Herbert, 1976 and Gregory, 1979; 1982). The attendance for each child was collected for the two terms and up till 1st July for the third term. The reading ages were provided by the remedial staff. For school A the test was not known: for

school B it was Schonell Test A (Schonell, 1965). The desire was to collect reasonably accurate and reliable data as efficiently as possible. From one's own observations it was realised that action-research could easily be bogged down at the assessment of need stage and never progress to any action or implementation of new practice.

RESULTS

Comparisons of pupil characteristics

Table 3.1: Socio-economic status

	Total	Class III or higher	Class IV	Class V	Unknown
School A	(N=123)	66.7%	11.4%	8.9%	13%
School B	(N=101)	40%	29%	20%	11%

Two-thirds of school A intake is Class III or higher whereas less than half that of school B is.

Table 3.2: Family size

	5 + children	3/4 children	2 or less children
School A	25.2%	29.3%	45.5%
School B	42%	33%	19% (7% unknown)

School B has approximately $1\frac{1}{2}$ times more children from large families than school A and fewer children from small families.

Table 3.3: Reading test attainments

	Reading Age 8 or less
School A	9%
School B	27%

School B has three times more poor readers (but remember that the reading test used in school A was not specified).

29

Table 3.4: Socially disadvantaged pupils

School A	12.2%
School B	21.0%

School B has more than $1\frac{1}{2}$ times the proportion of disadvantaged pupils compared to school A. Nationally 6% of 11-year-old pupils are from disadvantaged homes (Wedge and Prosser, 1973).

Table 3.5: Disadvantage and poor reading ability (RA of 8 or less)

School A	26%
School B	43%

Nearly half of the disadvantaged pupils in school B are poor readers whereas only a quarter of those in school A are poor readers.

Table 3.6: Living in a one-parent family

School A	13.8%
School B	26%

Table 3.7: Living with a large (5 or more children) or one-parent family

School A	35%
School B	59%

These figures compare with 23% of 11-year-old children who nationally live with a large or one-parent family (Wedge and Prosser, 1973).

The data in Tables 3.1, 3.2, 3.3, 3.4, 3.5, 3.6 and 3.7 indicate that though these schools are both comprehensive, of similar size and situated in the same district, they have a very different pupil intake (at least for 1976/77) which, if reflecting the position higher up the school, may generate problems with regard to courses the school might put on (for instance in school B three-quarters of its intake was below average in reading). Such findings raise the major question of what might be the best method of organising for teaching, groups of pupils which may vary in the proportion of high and low ability. It may be that different methods of organisation suit different groups. Gregory (1982) provides some tentative evidence to suggest that withdrawing pupils for remedial work from mixed ability classes may depress their school attendance.

Table 3.8: School attendance rates

Term 1 Attendance level	Percentage of pupils School A N = 123	School B girls N = 38
More than 90%	74%	76%
Between 75-90%	20%	13%
Less than 75%	6%	11%
Term 2	N = 123	N = 38
More than 90%	80%	50%
Between 75-90%	15%	24%
Less than 75%	5%	26%
Term 3	N = 123	N = 37
More than 90%	75%	51%
Between 75-90%	22%	22%
Less than 75%	3%	27%

Let us examine the attendance rates in the two schools. Only the girls of school B are considered in order to be comparable with school A - a girls' school. Table 3.8 indicates the proportion of children who attend for more than 90% of the time, between 75 and 90% and less than 75% of the time.

Looking at Table 3.8 and Figure 3.1, the attendance for girls in school A remains broadly constant whilst that of girls in school B starts from a similar point in the first term but shows that for terms two and three many more pupils are attending for less time.

These differences could be due to school B having many more socially disadvantaged pupils and such pupils tend to attend less well anyway (Galloway, 1976). When the attendance for each girl was rendered a percentage for the year (variable X) and social disadvantage (variable Y) is statistically rendered comparable using the analysis of covariance for both school A and school B, it was found that the mean attendance of girls at school A was significantly better (at the 2% level) than that of school B (see table 3.9).

Figure 3.1: Percentage of pupils attending for less than 90 per cent of the time

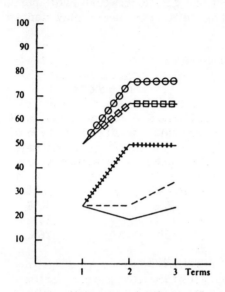

Key

—— School A all girls
––– School A remedial class girls
╫╫╫╫ School B all girls
ⓔⓔⓔ School B girls being withdrawn for English, maths and handwriting (N = 4)
▣▣▣ School B girls being withdrawn for English (N = 6)

Table 3.9

	School A N = 123	School B N = 37
Mean X	92.6	86.5*
Mean Y	1.8	2.8

* The difference between the means (analysis of covariance) is significant at the 0.02 level. F = 6.66 for degrees of freedom 1 and 157

X = attendance averaged over three terms for each pupil

Y = social disadvantage score for each pupil

Analysis of covariance (McNemar, 1962) was used to compare the attendance scores for school A with those of the girls in school B (i.e. two groups of unequal size) after making them comparable with respect to Y, the social disadvantage variable.

Thus even when one allows for the fact that school B has more socially disadvantaged girls, it still shows significantly poorer attendance levels for the first-year girls than school A.

Organisation differences between the schools may be a causal factor. In the first year school A had an upper and lower band of two classes in each and a small remedial class taught for about half the timetable by one remedial teacher, whilst school B had total mixed ability with withdrawal of some pupils for extra remedial help with any one of a number of teachers. This resulted in the lowest ability children being taught by the most teachers.

If one now examines the differences between the remedial girls in both schools, namely the remedial class of eleven children in school A and the six girls withdrawn for English in school B, one finds that these two groups are broadly comparable. In both cases the criterion for selection was having a reading age of eight years or less. Four girls or 36.3% were socially disadvantaged in the remedial class of school A whilst one or 16.7% of the withdrawn girls of school B was disadvantaged.

Comparing the attendances of these two groups (Table 3.10) shows that the girls of the remedial class in school A were significantly more likely to be good attenders (i.e. attending 90% or more over the year), than the withdrawn girls of school B.

Table 3.10: Remedial children

	School A N = 11		School B N = 6		
Poor attenders	3	A	B	5	A + B = 8
Good attenders	8	C	D	1	C + D
	A + C = 11		B + D = 6		

P = .042982

The remedial class of school A are compared to the girls withdrawn for English in school B for attendance. (Poor attendance is taken as attending for less than 90% of the time over the whole year.) Using Fisher's Exact probability (for N less than 20) Siegel (1956), we find that this table or one more extreme is likely to occur by chance less than 5% of the time.

This result cannot be blamed on social disadvantage since the withdrawn girls of school B having the poorer attendance have a lower and more favourable level of social disadvantage than the remedial class of school A. This variable is in the opposite direction to the attendance levels.

Figure 3.1 shows that not only do these girls withdrawn for English show poorer attendance than similar girls in a neighbouring school, they are poorer than the attendance of first-year girls in general in school B; those being withdrawn for most lessons showing the poorest attendance.

The difference in attendance of remedial girls in these two schools may be due to any number of factors, but one cannot avoid questioning whether it is due in part to the different ways the two schools organise these pupils.

CONCLUSION

School A has a significantly better level of attendance than school B even when the samples are rendered comparable for social disadvantage. The reason for this may be because school A is single sex or to do with the difference between the schools in (a) the way the pupils are grouped for teaching, (b) curriculum, (c) attitudes and consequences for non-attendance, (d) some other environmental or organisational factors.

Remedial girls in school A attend better than those withdrawn for English in school B.

Only two comprehensive schools have been compared and consequently the generalisability of the findings may be limited. What is generalisable is the principle of evaluation - what works in one school because of a particular set of circumstances may not work in another. It would seem imperative in these times of economic recession that schools evaluate their own procedures, systems and curricula to see their effect on pupils, staff and parents. Now, more than ever, teachers need to find out what works in their schools and what does not, and as a consequence believe in and institute systematic change and then monitor the results. It may be that the educational psychologist could provide an invaluable source of expertise in scientific evaluation. For example following this assessment of need, the findings for school B were discussed with the headteacher with a view to trying to improve the situation. Firstly one aspect of poor pupil attendance is the attitude of parents to the school. Because parents' evenings were poorly attended, attempts were made to improve the position and the changes evaluated. (Gregory, 1980 and 1981, Gregory, Meredith and Woodward, 1982).

Secondly first-year pupils were grouped in subsequent years with top, middle and two parallel remedial classes. A well-designed remedial reading programme for teenagers and adults (Corrective Reading published by Science Research Associates) was introduced on an experimental basis, and found to be much superior to the school's own remedial programme in accelerating reading progress. As an unexpected benefit the experimental group of children not only improved in reading but also showed better behaviour in other lessons and better school attendance over the year, than the control group. (Gregory, Hackney and Gregory, 1981 and 1982). This illustrates the steps of 'need assessment' followed by action-research and shows that change is possible in secondary schools and that it can be evaluated as a joint venture between staff at the school and the psychologist. There are many more schools than one would expect who are willing to experimentally evaluate current or new practice. Of all the different professions in education the LEA psychologist is probably in the best position, and with the most appropriate knowledge, to help such schools.

REFERENCES

Biddle, B.J. (1970) 'The institutional context.' W.J. Campbell (ed.) Scholars in Context: the effect of environments on learning. Chichester: John Wiley

Department of Education and Science (1977) 'Ten Good Schools: A secondary school enquiry'. HMI Series Matters of Discussion. London: HMSO

Galloway, D. (1976) 'Size of school, socioeconomic hardship, suspension rates and persistent unjustified absence from school'. British Journal of Educational Psychology, 6, 40-7

Gath, D., Cooper, B. and Gatton, I.F. (1972) Preliminary Communication. Child Guidance and Delinquency in a London Borough. Oxford University Press

Gregory, R.P. (1979) 'Using social disadvantage index in a secondary school.' Remedial Education, Vol. 14, No. 1, 5-11

Gregory, R.P. (1980) 'Disadvantaged parents and contact with secondary school.' Therapeutic Education, 8, 2, 23-6

Gregory, R.P. (1981) 'Parents' evenings, comprehensive schools, what are they for?' Comprehensive Education, 42, 24-5

Gregory, R.P. (1983) 'A secondary school's withdrawal system for helping pupils with remedial problems. An example of within-school evaluation.' Journal of Applied Educational Studies, 12, 1, 44-55

Gregory, R.P., Hackney, C. and Gregory, N.M. (1981) 'Corrective Reading Programme: The use of educational technology in a secondary school.' School Psychology International, Vol. 2, No. 2, 21-5

Gregory, R.P., Hackney, C. and Gregory, N.M. (1982) 'Corrective reading. An evaluation.' British Journal of Educational Psychology, 52, 33-50

Gregory, R.P., Meredith, P.T. and Woodward, A.M. (1982) 'Parent involvement in secondary school.' Association of Educational Psychologists' Journal, Vol. 5, 8, 54-60

Herbert, G.W. (1976) 'Social problems: Identification and action.' The Early Identification of Educationally 'at risk' Children, Wedell, K. and Reybould, E.C. (eds) Educational Review occasional paper No. 6: University of Birmingham

McDill, E.L., Myers, E.D. and Rigsby, K.C. (1974) 'Institutional effects on the academic behaviour of high school students.' Majoribanks, K. (ed.) Environments for Learning Windsor: NFER

McNemar, Q. (1962) Psychological Statistics. Chichester John Wiley

Reynolds, D. et al. (1974) 'Being absent from school.' British Journal Law and Society. 1, 78-81

Rutter, M. and Madge, N. (1976) Cycles of Disadvantage. London: Heinemann

Rutter, M., Maughan, B., Mortimore, P. and Ouston, J. (1979) Fifteen Thousand Hours, Secondary Schools and their Effects on Children. London: Open Books

Schonell, F.J. (1965) Backwardness in the Basic Subjects. London: Oliver and Boyd

Siegel, S. (1956) Nonparametic Statistics for the Behavioural Sciences. London: McGraw Hill

Tizard, J. (1974) 'The upbringing of other people's children, Implications of research.' Journal of Child Psychology and Psychiatry, 15, 161-73

Wedge, P. and Prosser, H. (1973) Born to Fail. National Children's Bureau. Arrow Books: London

Yule, W. and Rutter, M. (1976) unpublished data - quoted in Rutter, M. and Madge, N. (1976)

Chapter Four

TRUANCY: A PLAN FOR SCHOOL-BASED ACTION-RESEARCH*

INTRODUCTION

The intention of this paper is to propose a model and plan of research which a particular school might undertake, possibly in conjunction with a psychologist, in attempting to solve its own truancy problems. However, firstly let us briefly examine some of the findings, and the course, of educational research into truancy from school.

Much has been written about school phobia, truancy and absenteeism and a number of reviews of the literature are available (Carroll, 1977).

(a) Extent of the problem

Nationally overall attendance rates in schools are around 90% (Withrington 1975), but there are regional variations. 14.6% of children aged 11 in Wales were attending for less than 85% of school time, whereas the corresponding figure for South-West England was 7.5% (Davie et al., 1972 and Fogelman and Richardson 1974).

Absence from school can be justified or unjustified. Discovering whether a particular absence is one or the other is very difficult. N.A.C.E.W.O. (1975) estimated that 40% of absence from school was unjustified, and Reynolds and Murgatroyd (1974) put it as high as 75% (based on their investigation of absences in a single year in nine

* Reprinted by kind permission from the Journal of the Association of Educational Psychologists, 5, 3, 30-34, 1980

comprehensive schools).

(b) **Factors relating to absenteeism**

Reynolds and Murgatroyd (1977) suggest that past educational research has concentrated on examining the characteristics of persistently absent pupils and to some lesser extent their families, but rarely considered the schools from which they were absenting themselves. They go on to say:

> In part this neglect of the school situation of truanting children may reflect the inherent tendency of many psychologists turned educational researchers whose education has trained them to individualize the explanation of personal problems in terms of personal pathology. In part the neglect may spring from the fact that few of these authors were able to consider the schools their truants attended because of the nature of their research design. In part the neglect may spring from the reluctance of LEAs to permit careful assessment of their truants' schools.

Rarely, as Reynolds and Murgatroyd point out, have researchers given a definition for the absence to which they have addressed themselves even though truancy is legally defined in Section 39 of the 1944 Education Act. 'A truant is a child aged between 5 and 16 who fails to attend school and does not have a legitimate reason for being absent.'

The three 'acceptable' reasons for absence are: sickness or other unavoidable cause relating to the child, religious observances by a body to which the parents belong, if the school to which the child is registered is not within walking distance (3 miles or under by the nearest available route) and no suitable arrangements for his transportation are made by the LEA.

For the remainder of this paper this definition of truancy and unjustified absence will be used.

(c) **Characteristics of absentees**

Past psychological and educational research reveals an association between poor school attendance, backwardness in basic subjects, delinquency and socially disadvantaged families (Carroll, 1977).

(d) **Within-school factors relevant to absenteeism**

Consideration of the part school plays in pupil-behaviour has occurred only in the last few years. Most recently Rutter et al. (1979) in a comparison of inner London secondary schools found that their pupils differed markedly in attendance, delinquency rate and attainment, even when comparisons were restricted to children with similar home background and personal characteristics prior to secondary transfer. Secondary schools do shape the behaviour of their children. Similarly, Power, Benn and Morris (1972) found that some schools reduced, whereas others increased, a pupil's chance of being delinquent.

Reynolds (1976, 1977 and 1978) and Reynolds and Murgatroyd (1974) found large differences in attendance, delinquency and attainment between nine comprehensive schools. These differences could not be explained by differences in pupil-intake. In fact the schools with the more intelligent intake generally were worst on the above three measures. High rates of attendance were associated with the following factors within the schools: (a) enforcement of uniform in lower school, (b) operation of a prefect system, (c) minimal use of corporal punishment.

The rules operated by the schools tended to determine the extent of the absence rate.

Murgatroyd (1974, 1975a and b, 1977) and Lewis and Murgatroyd (1976), present material to support the contention that those comprehensive schools that admit to absenteeism problems, and which have a middle management pastoral care system (i.e. use of year tutors, house tutors and school counsellors), have de-emphasised the role of the school as an organisation in generating its own problems and diminished the role of the form tutor in pastoral care. Such schools are associated with poor rates of attendance, high rates of cautions for delinquency, high incidence of drug taking and poor academic output.

If the school is an important influence upon its own pupils' level of truancy, delinquency and educational failure, we should perhaps consider the direction of some of our current educational policies. When confronted by social problems like truancy, delinquency or so-called 'behavioural disorder' our automatic tendency has been, and still is, to appoint more educational psychologists, employ more advisers and introduce more school based social workers. A veritable army of members of the 'helping' professions now exist to 'help' - or rather force - the child to adjust to the reality of his school existence, irrespective of whether the reality is worth adjusting to' (Reynolds and Murgatroyd, 1977).

WITHIN-SCHOOL EVALUATION

There have been no published studies to date aimed at intervening to improve attendance in a high absenteeism school (Carroll, 1977). He only quotes one on-going action-research project involving South Glamorgan Education and Social Services Department, in which two teachers and a school counsellor as part of their brief are to explore the organisation of a school to see how it has an influence on truancy.

The thesis in this paper is that such action research should be part of a school's on-going activity. No organisation can be perfect but systematic evaluation of the behaviour of those who make up the organisation should provide essential feedback. It is suggested that efforts might be best concentrated on the first two years of comprehensive intake as Carroll (1977) finds that poor attenders in these early years of secondary school tend to be the poor attenders of the final years.

It would be impossible in such a school-based project to prove rigorously which variables have an effect on attendance. Even in well-designed experiments, extraneous variables often intrude, and reduce the generalisation of results and conclusions (Burroughs, 1970). All available attempts must be made to improve attendance at a given time, whilst monitoring the attendance rates in the hope that some hypotheses will be rendered more tenable than others. Where possible a control group, or at least two groups, should be used.

A MODEL FOR PLANNING AND EVALUATING ACTION RESEARCH

Ainscow, Bond, Gardner and Tweddle (1978) have described the following model in detail for the planning and evaluation of in-service training courses for teachers. However it is considered equally valuable in the process of planning and evaluation in other areas - namely departmental meetings (Gregory and Tweddle, 1978), and these could include action-research.

Figure 4.1: The model

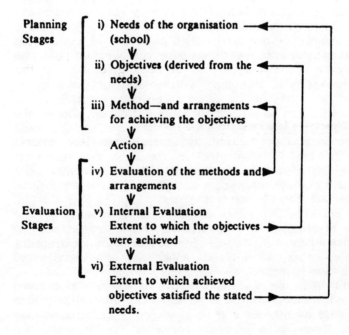

Planning Stages

i) Needs of the organisation (school)

ⅴ

ii) Objectives (derived from the needs)

ⅴ

iii) Method—and arrangements for achieving the objectives

ⅴ

Action

ⅴ

iv) Evaluation of the methods and arrangements

ⅴ

Evaluation Stages

v) Internal Evaluation
Extent to which the objectives were achieved

ⅴ

vi) External Evaluation
Extent to which achieved objectives satisfied the stated needs.

As can be seen this model could probably be applied to any action-research activity. It comprises a sequence of three planning stages and three corresponding levels of evaluation. The model is based on the 'systems approach' and on behavioural objectives. Their use is largely restricted to work with the mentally handicapped, although increasingly they are being applied in a range of different contexts (James 1976, Golby et al., 1975 and Ainscow and Tweddle 1977).

The remainder of this paper is presented within the framework of the six aspects of the model.

PLANNING STAGE

(i) The needs of the school

At this point one is asking about the needs of the school and this could include reference to those of parents, staff and pupils. In this context an increase in pupil attendance and the testing of hypotheses concerning the school factors having an influence on attendance rate are seen as the needs. This general statement of need gives rise to the second stage.

(ii) Objectives (derived from the needs)

The needs lead on to aims and goals. These are general statements of intended activity which it is decided are relevant to satisfying the stated needs. For example, goals derived from the following aim, 'to improve the attendance of some pupils' might be:

(1) to review the literature in search of factors relevant to absenteeism - that are under the control of the school
(2) to gather information about socially disadvantaged and potentially non-attending children in the school
(3) to consider ways of improving the pastoral care system
(4) to increase parental involvement in the school. The literature suggests that most of the unjustified absence is known to the parents (Galloway 1976, N.A.C.E.W.O. 1975). It would seem logical to hypothesise that the parent-school contact may be a factor in unjustified absence
(5) to involve teachers (possibly in lower school initially) in the aims, goals and objectives of the project and

43

increase their awareness of variables within and outside of their control that may influence attendance

(6) to examine the system of grouping pupils for teaching. Gregory (1979) found that the method of grouping pupils may be associated with their rate of attendance

(7) to consider the suitability of curriculum materials for pupils of different reading ability. Classes where the mismatch between the readability of text material and the child's reading ability is high tend to have high non-attendance rates

(8) to consider ways of improving fifth year attendance. Galloway (1976) found that secondary school absence was largely made up of the absence of fifth year pupils

(9) to consider ways of improving the school and E.W.O.'s procedures involved with absent children

(10) to examine the methods of working of the school E.W.O.

(11) to examine possible actions and techniques for returning non-attending children to school.

Those are some of the range of goals that could be derived from the needs and aims. We now must make the goals concrete by deriving a set of objectives for each goal. The value of objectives is that they are precise descriptions of observable behaviour. In teaching they describe what a pupil is expected to do following a learning activity. For action-research they will describe either what it is staff or personnel will be able to do following a teaching course (Ainscow, Bond, Gardner and Tweddle, 1978) - or what the researcher, target staff, parents or pupils do in observable terms to satisfy the aims and goals of the research. The objective requires a verb which describes an observable action.

Objectives derived from Goal 1:

1 - (i)   after having read some of the recent literature which reviews factors relevant to absenteeism, lists not less than five within-school factors.

1 - (ii) after completion of (i) lists not less than five within-school variables which it is hypothesised may be factors in unjustified absenteeism from the target school.

Both of these objectives have (a) verbs denoting observable

actions, i.e. lists, (b) conditions - i.e. in 1 - (i) 'after having read some recent literature' and (c) a criterion level, i.e. the list must not be less than five variables.

Objectives dervied from Goal 2:

2 - (i)   produces a data sheet which collects the following information during initial interview with parents of prospective first-year pupils: one-parent family, father's (or mother's if one-parent family) occupation, number of children in the family, receipt of free school meals, etc. This information can be used to measure the extent of social disadvantage in the child's home situation. (For further details see Herbert (1976) and Gregory (1979)).

2 - (ii)   for all first-year pupils for the first term, calculates and lists the percentage attendance and whether absence is considered unjustified. Carroll (1977) found that poor attenders in the first year, i.e. less than 85% attendance in the first term, tended to be poor attenders in later years.

2 - (iii)   lists the children identified as at-risk of being poor attenders through the use of the social disadvantage index and attendance rating for the first term.

Objectives derived from Goal 3:

3 - (i)   lists the workings of the present pastoral care system.

3 - (ii)   incorporates as many as possible of factors and variables identified in objectives 1 (i) and (ii) into the pastoral care system.

3 - (iii)   passes form teachers a list of potential (and actual) poor attenders identifed in objective 2 (iii).

3 - (iv)   asks form teachers to attempt to form a positive relationship, particularly with potential (or actual) poor attenders, by at least praising any achievement and attendance.

3 - (v)   that form teachers of potential (or actual) poor attenders visit the parents of these pupils by the end of the first term - to indicate the positive

aspect of the child's progress and to reinforce the parents for their efforts in gaining the present progress.

3 - (vi) lists the workings of the improved pastoral care system.

3 - (vii) writes down and implements a competition between classes for the best attendance level, with appropriate rewards for the winning class.

3 - (viii) writes down and implements a scheme in which persistent non-attenders are rewarded for improved attendance and such that their class as a whole as a consequence, gains privileges and the pupils' parents are informed of progress. (Here one is utilising peers as therapeutic agents in changing the inappropriate behaviour of target pupils (O'Leary and O'Leary, 1972). The peers are likely to reinforce target pupils for improved attendance.)

Objectives derived from Goal 4:

4 - (i) writes down a date for parents of possibly prospective first-year pupils to visit the school on an open evening in order to see the school, understand its aims and thus make a more rational choice of secondary school. The evening could be advertised via the feeder primary schools.

4 - (ii) increases the number of parents attending parents' evenings.

4 - (iii) increases the number of parents active in the parents' association.

4 - (iv) lists the number of school events to which parents are invited.

4 - (v) produces and circulates three booklets (1) telling parents of new pupils the aims of the school, school rules, teaching staff, school arrangements, etc., (2) telling parents of options at third-year level, C.S.E., 'O' level and the implications for careers, (3) outlining sixth form courses and the implications for careers and further education courses.

5 - (i) organises and implements a set of seminars for staff that (1) describe the project, (2) teaches them the principles of teaching to objectives and behavioural management.

6 - (i)   compares the attendance of classes within years.

7 - (i)   discusses the possibility of the remedial teacher spending most of his time devising suitable curriculum material for remedial pupils in conjunction with other heads of departments.

7 - (ii)   measures the readability of text books used and removes any major discrepancies between those scores and the reading age of pupils using the books.

7 - (iii)   evalutes a reading curriculum of known value with remedial pupils in the school - comparing it to the existing provision.

8 - (i)   discusses Goal 8 with staff and lists changes to be undertaken.

9 - (i)   after examining the existing procedures for absent pupils lists any changes necessary.

10 - (i)   lists (a) the number of E.W.O.s serving the school.

        (b)   the basis on which they get their caseload and the weekly number.

        (c)   the criteria and numbers involved for who is:

        (i)   visited

        (ii)   taken to committee

        (iii)   taken to court.

10 - (ii)   sets up an experiment to find out whether children visited by the E.W.O. return to school quicker or show subsequent improved attendance over a control group not visited. (Carroll, 1977, finds in his review of the literature, that no evaluation of the effects of E.W.O. or social worker visits to poor attenders has ever been done.)

11 - (i)   after reviewing the literature on intervention for persistent non-attenders produces an 'action pack' for returning such children back to school which could be used by E.W.O.s. (Such an action pack might include a financial assessment re. welfare benefits, and behavioural techniques applicable to the family child and school when the child returns.)

(iii) **Method and arrangements for achieving the objective(s)**
Each of these objectives from 1(i) to (iii) must now be achieved by various methods. One would hope to select the

method which would most efficiently achieve the objective. Different methods may suit different objectives. It would be tedious to discuss every objective according to each of the remaining stages of the model - thus, just two objectives will be examined in this way. Consider objective 1(i). The method may involve one member of staff, a small committee or the educational psychologist in doing the task. However, to achieve objective 3(ii) major changes in the pastoral care system may be necessary and a set of meetings of senior staff and form teachers to discuss possible arrangements may be the optimal method. It is at this point that an experimental design may be considered e.g. the new system may be applied to one set of classes and not another to see whether any difference in attendance rate or behaviour (Burroughs, 1970) between the two sets of classes occur.

The planning stages are now complete and the activity can be put into operation. In short we have asked: what are the needs, what objectives might satisfy these needs, what methods appear to be most likely to efficiently achieve these objectives?

EVALUATION

(iv) **Evaluation of method and arrangements**
This is the point at which one would review the method used. It may be for example that (objective 1 (i)) the use of a small committee took a great deal of time and staff were not happy with it. Another arrangement might have been better. One can only find out the best method by trying something and then monitoring the effect. For objective 3(ii) the following questions would not be asked: were the appropriate staff invited to the meetings, was the time, length of meeting and work sharing appropriate?

(v) **Internal evaluation**
Has the objective been achieved? If so, one can proceed to the final stage.

(vi) **External evaluation**
To what extent have the achieved objectives satisfied the stated needs? This question is less appropriate for objective

1(i) than for 3(ii). At the end of a trial period one might compare attendance rates of pupils on the new pastoral care system with a control group. Such a comparison would not prove without doubt that the new system was better, but it may produce results which make such a hypothesis more tenable. If the effect was monitored for a further period, evidence would accumulate to strengthen or weaken the hypothesis. One would be a little clearer as to whether one's activities in school were helping to satisfy the perceived needs.

In short the evaluation stages ask: to what extent have the methods used helped the achievement of the objective? has the objective been achieved? (Since the objective was written in observable terms this question can now be readily answered.) Has the achieved objective helped satisfy the perceived need? (It may or may not have.)

CONCLUSION

This model may at first sight appear complex, but such planning and evaluation may avoid the gap between the needs of schools and the research objectives pursued by educational academics. The pre-requisites for such an operation are only, (a) a school with staff willing to examine their own behaviour and school structures to see the effect these have on pupils and staff and, (b) possibly some help from a school psychological service.

Some headteachers already collect feedback information about the effect of various school arrangements in an informal way. This model just formalises this good practice.

It would seem essential to change within-school variables before setting up special units for children presenting as a problem. As an illustration the South Glamorgan Secondary School Project (Carroll, 1977 p. 28) found a truancy centre unnecessary in a school where 50% of second-year pupils were poor attenders, after within-school changes were made.

REFERENCES

Ainscow, M., Bond, J., Gardner, J. and Tweedle, D.A. (1978) 'The development of a three part evaluation procedure for inset course'. British Journal of In-Service Education, 4, No 3. 184-90

Ainscow, M. and Twedle, D.A. (1977) 'Behavioural objectives and children with learning difficulties'. Association of Educational Psychologists Journal, Vol. 4, 5, 33-7

Burroughs, G.E.R. (1970) Design and Analysis in Educational Research. Education Monograph, University of Birmingham

Carroll, H.C.M. (ed.) (1977) Absenteeism in South Wales Studies of Pupils, their Homes and their Secondary Schools. Faculty of Education, University of Swansea

Davie, R., Butler, N. and Goldstein, H. (1972) From Birth to Seven. London: Longman

Education Act (1944) London: H.M.S.O.

Fogelman, K. and Richardson, K. (1974) 'School attendance: Some results from the National Child Development Study.' Turner, B. (ed.) (1974) Truancy. London: Ward Lock Educational

Galloway, D. (1976) 'Size of school, socio-economic hardship suspension rates and persistent unjustified absence from school.' British Journal of Educational Psychologists, Vol. 46, 1, 40-7

Golby, M., Greenwood, J. and West, R. (eds) (1975) Curriculum Development. London: Croom Helm

Gregory, R.P. (1979) 'Using a social disadvantage index in a secondary school.' Remedial Education, Vol. 14, No. 1, 5-11

Gregory, R.P. and Tweedle, D.A. (1978) 'Planning and evaluating meetings.' Social Work Service, No. 16, 21-5

Herbert, G.W. (1976) 'Social problems: Identification and action.' Early Identification of Educationally 'at risk' Children. Wedell, K. and Raybould, E.C. (eds) Educational Review No. 6, University of Birmingham

James, R. (1976) 'Management by objectives.' Social Work Today, Vol. 6, No. 21, 655-7

Lewis, G. and Murgatroyd, S.J. (1976) 'The professional-isation of counselling in education and its legal implications.' British Journal of Guidance Counselling 4, 1, 2-15

Murgatroyd, S.J. (1974) 'Ethical issues in secondary school counselling.' Journal of Moral Education, 4, 1, 27-37

Murgatroyd, S.J. (1975a) 'The psychologist, the sociologist and the truant.' New Psychologist, 1, 1, 3-18

Murgatroyd, S.J. (1975b) 'School-centred counselling.' New Era, 56, 4, 90-1

Murgatroyd, S.J. (1977) 'Pupil perceptions of counsellors'.
British Journal of Guidance Counselling, 5, 1
National Association of Chief Education Welfare Officers
(1975) 'Those we serve: the report of a working party
set up to enquire into the causes of absence from
school.' Bedford: National Association of Chief
Education Welfare Officers
O'Leary, K.D. and O'Leary, S.G. (1972) 'The effects of peers
as therapeutic agents in the classroom.' K.D. O'Leary
and S.G. O'Leary, Classroom Management. The
Successful need of Behaviour Modification. Oxford:
Pergamon
Power, M.J., Benn, R.T. and Morris, J.N. (1972) 'Neighbour-
hood school and juveniles before the Courts.' British
Journal of Criminology 12, 2, 111-32
Reynolds, D. (1976) 'Schools do make a difference.' New
Society, 37, 720, 223-5
Reynolds, D. (1977) 'The delinquent school.' Hammersley, N.
and Woods, P. (eds) The Process of Schooling. London:
Routledge, Kegan and Paul
Reynolds, D. (1978) Schools Do Make a Difference London:
Routledge Kegan Paul
Reynolds, D. and Murgatroyd, S.J. (1974) 'Being absent from
school.' British Journal of the Law Society, 1, 1, 78-81
Reynolds, D. and Murgatroyd, S.J. (1977) 'The sociology of
schooling and the absent pupil. The school as a factor in
the generation of truancy'. Carroll, H.C.M. (ed.) op. cit.
Rutter, M., Maughan, B., Mortimore, P. and Ouston, J.
(1979) Fifteen Thousand Hours. Secondary Schools and
their effects on children. London: Open Books
Withrington, D. (1975) 'Anxieties over withdrawal from
school: historical comment'. Research Intelligence, 20-2

Chapter Five

PARENTS' EVENINGS IN COMPREHENSIVE SCHOOLS: WHAT ARE THEY FOR?

INTRODUCTION

Attendance rates at parents' evenings appear to vary from school to school, but it is not unusual to find only 20-30% of pupils represented at such evenings.

The reasons for these low figures are likely to be numerous and vary according to the school.

However, the intention of this paper is to put forward a model and some considerations for the planning and evaluation of a parents' evening with the aim of increasing the attendance. This model could probably be applied to other systems and activities within the school.

Such a project would appear, at first sight, simplistic, but it raises at least three issues.

The first is that of research and evaluation in education. In the past it would probably be true to say that educational research has been directed towards finding principles which are generalisable across education, but as Tizard 1976 indicates there has been little evaluation of actual practice; little within-school evaluation.

It is likely that schools could be encouraged to ask themselves whether their activities gain the objectives they set out to achieve. Such questions are being asked of other areas of education: namely in-service training courses for teachers (Taylor, 1977).

The second issue is that of parent-involvement in the secondary school. (Watkins and Derrick 1977 provide useful

*Based on a paper which appeared in Comprehensive Education, 42, 24-5, 1981

52

references to work in this area.) It is hypothesised that a greater awareness amongst parents of the aims of a school and the achievements of their children would aid the school in its endeavours. One aspect of parent-involvement is their attendance at parents' evenings in school.

Thirdly, the work of educational psychologists in school psychological services has largely been restricted to dealing with individual referrals of children presenting as a problem. It is hoped that this paper indicates how psychology might be applied to problems at a level above that of individual children, but whose solution would reflect on many of the pupils in the school.

Psychologists in future, may well have a role, in partnership with senior staff, in promoting within-school evaluation.

Figure 5.1: A model for planning and evaluating a parents' evening

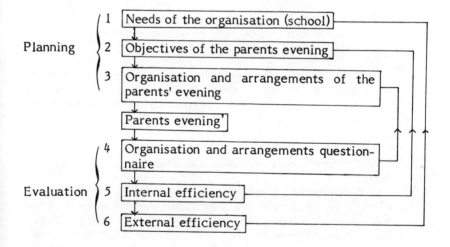

This model has been suggested for use in planning and evaluating meetings (Gregory and Tweddle, 1978) and in-service training courses for teachers (Ainscow, Bond, Gardner and Tweddle, 1978).

It comprises a sequence of three planning stages and three corresponding levels of evaluation.

PLANNING STAGES

(1)   The needs of the organisation
What are the needs of the school that might be met by having a Parents' Evening?

It is suggested that increased parental-involvement in the school is the need and with this might come a clearer understanding for staff, parents and pupils of the aims, goals and objectives of the school. Such clarity might have an effect on school attendance, pupil commitment to achievement and parental cooperation, etc.

(2)   Objectives of the parents' evening
What behavioural objectives will meet the stated needs?

The use of objectives in education is an advanced technology especially in the American literature. Their use in Britain is still largely restricted to work with the mentally handicapped, although increasingly they are being applied in a range of different contexts. Stenhouse (1975), Golby et al. (1975) and Ainscow and Tweddle (1977) provide useful references for readers who wish to pursue the subject further.

Behavioural objectives are precise descriptions of observable behaviour. In education they usually describe what a pupil is expected to do following a learning activity. For a parents' evening they will describe what the parents will be able to to do by the end of the evening as a consequence of having attended. We must ask 'what do we want the parents to learn through attending the parents' evening?' If we do not know what we want to teach them we will not know whether we have been successful

Some objectives for a parents' evening might be:

(1)   that more parents attend than on previous occasions.

(2) that the parents by the end of the evening should be able to write down when asked:

(a) some of their child's positive achievements in each subject in the last term.
(b) what their child next needs to learn in each subject.
(c) positive aspects of their child's general behaviour in school.
(d) the positive behaviour he needs to learn in school.

(A criticism of this set of objectives is that it may require much time for parents to be taught to achieve these, within one evening. It may be that lower level objectives are necessary initially. This could be done by altering the wording e.g. 'some subjects' instead of 'each'. Alternatively they could be rewritten as, 'the parents should be able to write down, when asked, whether their child is making progress or not in some subjects'.)

(3) That parents should meet and talk with as many of their child's teachers as possible.
(4) That the parents should be able to write down, when asked:

(a) some of the school's aims, goals and objectives for the pupils.
(b) that school attendance is relevant to their child's progress in school.
(c) that the procedure when their child is absent is to send a note with the child when he returns or phone/visit the school.

(5) that parents talk with as many other parents as possible.
(6) that a particular teacher should write down any family, medical or physical changes for the pupil relevant to his behaviour in school.

Parents' evenings for pupils of different years could have different objectives. For example, an evening for parents of third-year pupils may be concerned with introducing options to be decided in the fourth year and the implications for future careers.

The discerning reader may notice that the above

objectives could be achieved using an arrangement other than a parents' evening.

(3)   Organisation and arrangements of the
      parents' evening
      What are the optimal conditions for achieving
      the objectives?

It is only after the objectives have been clearly stated that one can consider the method (or organisation and arrangements) by which they might be achieved. The following sample of questions needs to be answered at this level of planning.

Who should attend - first or second-year parents? Which staff are needed - just form teachers or all subject teachers? Where should it be held - main hall or in classrooms? What is the best date and time, etc?

None of these questions can be answered without constant and specific reference to each of the evening's objectives.

Below are listed some of the arrangements which might achieve the above objectives. In places decisions have involved the application of another aspect of behavioural theory. This states that appropriate behaviour which is followed by rewarding consequences is likely to increase in frequency.

1.   The arrangements for the actual evening could involve the parents being welcomed, informed of the teachers' seating plan and the location of facilities.

2.   Consideration could be given to making the evening comfortable for the staff involved. If staff are punished by the experience they may not be so cooperative for the next evening event.

3.   Some of the pupils' books, and the register, could be available for parents to see.

4.   Select sixth-form pupils, a room, toys, etc. for a creche.

(Wedge and Prosser, 1973 found in a national survey that 23% of children were from one-parent or large families. The percentage will vary from area to area, but it may be that many parents cannot easily attend a parents' evening because of difficulties over baby sitting. A creche for pre-school children may help increase attendance. Other children possibly could remain with their parents at the evening, if no other arrangement could be made.)

5.   An arrangement whereby sixth-form pupils would baby sit for parents could be considered.

6.   Arrange a raffle and a draw half-way through the evening. The prizes could be gift vouchers from Boots or Smiths. This might be an added incentive for parents to attend the evening.

7.   Select the most suitable evening with regard to T.V. programmes and staff commitments with which one may be competing.

8.   Select the most suitable time with regard to parents getting home from work, having tea, and staff returning to school, etc.

9.   Consider having an exhibition of pupils' work on show.

10.   Design a letter to parents advertising the evening to be sent via the pupils, and to indicate

(a)   the objectives of the evening
(b)   date, time, place
(c)   details of creche or baby sitting facility, coffee and raffle
(d)   a tear-off slip to indicate parents' likelihood of attendance (but also as a check they received the letter) and need for creche or baby sitter
(e)   that if parents cannot attend then an adult son/daughter or near relative could come
(f)   pupils could accompany a parent only if the parent would otherwise be unable to attend.

The letter could be written in a positive welcoming easy-to-read style, with the aim of 'selling' the idea of attending.

With the letter could be sent a list of the child's teachers and subjects so that parents will be able to decide in advance who they wish to see.

11.   Each class of pupils involved could design a poster in the art lesson to advertise the parents' evening. The best poster from each class could be displayed in that classroom.

12.   Fifth and sixth-form art students could be invited to design a similar poster - the best of which could be displayed in the corridors and on school notice boards.

13.   Arrange a competition between the classes involved, such that the class gaining the highest percentage of parental attendance wins housepoints or a rewarding

activity. This is utilising pupil influence with parents in the same way that peers can be used as therapeutic agents in changing the inappropriate behaviour of target pupils (O'Leary and O'Leary, 1972).

14.   The school educational welfare officer (E.W.O.) could pass an advertising sheet to parents he visits in the course of his work. The sheet would remind parents of the evening. The E.W.O. could indicate how staff would be interested and pleased to see parents and generally extol the virtues of the evening.

15.   Design a simple questionnaire for parents to complete to see which objectives have been achieved and which arrangements suited them best.

16.   The staff involved should meet prior to the parents' evening. Such a meeting could have the following objectives. To acquaint staff

(a)   with the objectives and arrangements for the evening

(b)   with the proposal that staff should
   (i)   be positively reinforcing to the parents and indicate some positive achievements of the child in each subject, his general behaviour (e.g. punctuality, appearance, etc.) and the next steps in learning that subject.
   (ii)   indicate how the parents can help their child at home by praising progress, completion of homework and by being interested in his education and the implications for his career.
   (iii)   check to see whether there has been any significant change in the child's family situation or medical/physical well-being (e.g. vision, hearing, epilepsy, medication, etc.) that may have a bearing on behaviour in school. (To be discussed by one teacher only.)
   (iv)   indicate to the parents the relevance of good school attendance to school progress, and remind them of the procedure when absent. (To be discussed by one teacher.)
   (v)   end the interview on a positive note. If the parents are sufficiently reinforced by teachers they may attend subsequent evenings. There is no point in punishing a

parent so much that he never sets foot in the school again.

(vi) ask each parent to complete and return the simple questionnaire explaining that it is to find out the best way of arranging the evening to suit parents.

(vii) 'sell' the parents' evening to their pupils and describe the competition between classes for the highest attendance of parents at the evening.

(viii) aim to point out a pupil's good work and say it will be particularly mentioned or shown to his parents, and to avoid threatening pupils with adverse comments that staff will tell a child's parents. Such threats may cause the child to convince his parents not to attend.

A sequence of planning decisions has been proposed which can be summarised by the following questions.

(1) What practical needs are hoped to be achieved by holding the parents' evening?

(2) What behavioural objectives will meet these needs?

(3) What are the optimum arrangements for achieving these objectives?

Some suggestions have been made as to possible objectives and arrangements.

EVALUATION STAGES

(4) Organisation and arrangements
Can arrangements be improved which may help achieve more objectives quicker?

There are an infinite number of ways of organising a parents' evening. The question is, which arrangements serve best to achieve the objectives? One can only find this out by noting how many objectives are achieved when various arrangements are used. One can also ask parents and staff whether arrangements suited them. This could be done using a simple questionnaire in which a positive statement for each arrangement decision could be rated on a three-point scale, e.g.

	Agree		Disagree
'The starting time was convenient'	1	2	3

One could send a questionnaire via the pupils to a sample of parents who <u>did not attend</u> asking similar questions including the viability of alternatives to a parents' evening.

(5)   Internal efficiency
How many of the objectives for the parents' evening have been achieved?

A second section on the questionnaire could ask the parents to demonstrate in some way their knowledge for each objective. One would probably find that some objectives were achieved by some parents. This would indicate how successful the evening had been in getting over to parents the information considered important. If no objectives were set, one could not judge how successful one had been.

(6)   External efficiency
Did the parents' evening help meet the needs of the school?

Here we must refer back to Section 1 to see what needs might be satisfied by such an evening. The most obvious is the effect on attendance levels. Do the children of parents who attended the evening show subsequent improved attendance? Do these parents follow the procedure for absence more often than other parents? Are there fewer misunderstandings and conflicts between school and these parents? These statements are what Burroughs (1970) calls vague research hypotheses. They must be converted into statistical hypotheses before they can be tested.

A sequence of three levels of evaluation has been proposed which can be summarised by the following questions.

(1)   Can arrangements (even consider alternatives to parents' evenings) be improved which may help achieve more objectives quicker?

(2)   How many of the objectives were achieved by how

many parents?

(3) Given that some objectives are achieved, does the parents' evening help meet the needs of the school?

CONCLUSION

A model for planning and evaluating school activities with particular reference to parents' evenings has been described in some detail. It is suggested that this model facilitates planning and incorporates a system of evaluation.

If there is no evaluation there is no evidence to indicate that a system is working as it was intended.

If it does not work - why continue doing it?

REFERENCES

Ainscow, M., Bond, J., Gardner, J. and Tweddle, D. (1978) 'The development of a three part evaluation procedure for inset courses.' British Journal of In-Service Education, 4, 3, 184-90

Ainscow, M. and Tweddle, D. (1977) 'Behavioural objectives and children with learning difficulties'. Association of Educational Psychologists Journal, Vol. 4 and 5, 33-7

Burroughs, G.E.R. (1970) Design and Analysis in Educational Research. Education Monograph, University of Birmingham

Golby, M., Greenwood, J. and West, R. (eds) (1975) Curriculum Development. London: Croom Helm

Gregory, R.P. and Tweddle, D. (1978) 'Planning and evaluating meetings.' Social Work Service, 16, 21-5

O'Leary, D. and O'Leary, S. (1972) Classroom Management: The successful use of behaviour modification. Oxford: Pergamon Press

Stenhouse, L. (1975) An Introduction to Curriculum Research and Development. London: Heinemann

Taylor, P. (1977) 'Evaluating in-service training programmes.' Trends in Education. No. 3, 6-11

Tizard, J. (1976) 'Psychology and social policy.' Bulletin of the British Psychological Society. No. 29, 225-34

Watkins, R. and Derrick, D. (1977) Cooperative Care. Practice and information profiles. Manchester: Centre for information and advice on educational disadvantage

Wedge, P. and Prosser, H. (1973) Born to Fail? London:

Arrow Books/National Children's Bureau

Chapter Six

PARENTAL INVOLVEMENT IN SECONDARY SCHOOLS*

R. P. Gregory, P. Meredith and A. Woodward

SUMMARY

A framework for planning and evaluating Parents' Evenings is described. Its implementation resulted in a significantly greater home-school contact than had previously prevailed. Parental contact was found to be associated with pupil attainment and school attendance. However parents of remedial children did show a marked increase in contact with the school as a result of the project. Further suggestions for improving parent involvement are discussed.

INTRODUCTION

In recent years there has been a growing interest in the involvement of parents in their children's education. It has long been known that the children of parents concerned for education tend to do better at school than those of parents who are not. Often cited are the children of 'socially deprived families'. They tend to benefit least of all from schooling. Even when there is a major educational input for 'disadvantaged' children in enrichment programmes and higher achievement is produced, the fading-out phenomenon is common. Namely the children's achievements fall off once the programme has ended. Stickney (1978) in his review of three such programmes concluded that the cumulative deficit in disadvantaged children's attainment could be

*Reprinted by kind permission from the Journal of the Association of Educational Psychologists, 5, 8, 54-60, 1982

attributed largely to different experiences outside the school and not to learning rates during school. He points out the stimulation and facilities that children from advantaged homes get after school and during the holidays. These sorts of findings have led to efforts to increase the involvement of parents, particularly those who are disadvantaged, in the schooling of their children. Thus, all of the May 1978 issue of 'Disadvantage in Education', was devoted to parental involvement in primary schools. Fryer (1973) lists many ideas with an estimate of their effectiveness for improving contacts between home and school.

Other interventions have included reports from school to home. In Belgium a 'journal de classe' listing each day's lessons, homework and teachers' messages keeps the parent in daily touch with the school (Wilby, 1978). Dougherty and Dougherty (1977) describe other report card systems.

Parental contacts with their children's secondary schools have been examined by Bynner (1974). Parents (approximately 3,000) were asked whether they had talked to the head of their child's present school when he started.

Although most parents had visited the head of the child's primary school (with little difference between parents of different social classes), far fewer working class parents had done so at secondary school. To take the two extremes, contact of this kind actually increased for middle class parents to just over 80% visiting, whereas only 40% of parents in the unskilled manual group visited.

Parents who have not had the benefit of extended education are not as well-equipped to help their children with school work as parents who have had this advantage. Bynner suggests this puts an even greater responsibility on the schools in their teaching. However the very group of parents in the survey, who appeared to need help most had least contact with schools. Bynner found that schools varied in their provision of school functions to which parents were invited (Lynch and Pimlot, 1976, have similar findings). More working class than middle class parents were dissatisfied with what schools were providing for them. They wanted more information from the school about their child's progress and would have welcomed more contact with the teachers, particularly home visits (Bynner, 1974).

Bynner raises the question of what schools can do to improve home-school contacts. Firstly, Jones (1976) describes how reports at her school are not sent out, but instead parents are invited up to the school to read and discuss what the teachers have to say. In lower school some 80% of parents respond and this provides an opportunity for positive interchange. Pupil school-attendance was a problem in the lower school particularly in the first year. Jones reports great improvement following the implementation of this and other measures.

Secondly, Lynch and Pimlot (1976) in a Schools Council research study specifically sought ways of improving the home-school relations in three schools with particular focus on parents living in poorer areas.

Highlighting these problems one of the study-schools set in an inner city area with 16% of pupils on free dinners (a measure of the disadvantage) had open days for which parental attendance was practically nil and a parent association which became defunct through lack of support. When a parent group was formed for the purposes of the research study it was done by face to face invitation. These parents reported they liked meeting other parents and many supported the idea of teachers visiting them at home. The results indicated an association between parent contact with school, parental satisfaction, pupils' liking for school and good pupil attendance. Parental contact and satisfaction with the secondary school may well influence the child's view of school and his behaviour as measured by attendance. These associations occurred for all three schools, including the one in the inner city with high numbers of disadvantaged children. These and the findings of Jones (1976) are heartening. They support the view that even in the most apparently desperate situations schools can bring about significant changes themselves. It was with this optimism in mind that the authors of this paper came together to examine some of their concerns and embark on this project.

PARENTS' EVENING PROJECT

The improvement of the parental contact with the school was one of the goals listed in a discussion paper on school non-attendance and truancy developed out of the authors' joint work (Gregory, 1980). Following further consultation it was decided to particularly focus on the problem of poorly attended parents' evenings as one aspect of parent involvement. Many staff gave up their own time to prepare for such evenings only to find that very few parents availed themselves of the facility. A framework for the project was developed to include an evaluation (Gregory, 1981).

A FRAMEWORK FOR PLANNING AND EVALUATING THE PROJECT

Figure 6.1, described in detail in Gregory (1979a), owes its origins to Ainscow, Bond, Gardner and Tweddle (1978).

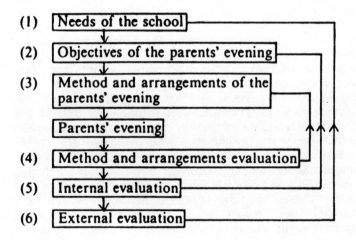

The remainder of this paper will be described within the context of this framework.

PLANNING STAGE 1 - NEEDS OF THE SCHOOL

What are the needs of the school that might be
met by having a Parents' Evening?

The school is a mixed comprehensive with three years of
comprehensive intake. It is situated in a suburb of a city in
the West Midlands consisting mainly of council housing and
very few owner-occupied houses. It has four-form intake and
approximately 630 pupils. Something of the type of
information about the catchment area of the school,
recommended by the Schools Council Report (1970) to be
collected prior to embarking on a home-school relations
project, was gathered in an earlier study. In this survey of
all the first-year pupils in year 1976/77, 60% were from
one-parent or large families (five or more children) as
compared to 23% nationally (Wedge and Prosser, 1973); 21%
were from socially disadvantaged homes (gaining five or
more points on an index of disadvantage - Herbert, 1976)
compared to 6% nationally for 11-year-old children (Wedge
and Prosser, 1973). They in fact used a different index of
disadvantage from Herbert (1976) and thus the comparisons
are tentative. It seemed reasonable to assume that children
from forms higher up the school would probably reflect a
similar social picture.

The pupils of the first three years are arranged into a
top and middle form with two parallel remedial classes in
each year. The fourth and fifth years are arranged in two
bands for each year.

A parent teachers' association was formed in November
1977 and has since arranged a number of successful
functions.

A general impression from senior staff of low
attendances at parents' evenings lead to the view that
improved parental contact with school was a major need and
that this might be tackled initially by endeavouring to
increase attendance at parents' evenings. It was considered
that greater home-school contact might lead to a clearer
understanding by parents, pupils and staff of the aims of the
school. Such clarity might have an effect on pupil
attendance at school, pupil commitment to achievement and
parental cooperation, etc.

A baseline measure of the attendance at January 1978
parents' evenings was taken and this confirmed the general
impression.

Table 6.1: A comparison of attendance at the January 1978 and July 1978 parents' evenings for 1st, 2nd, 3rd and 4th years

Attendance at Parents' Evening

	January 1978	July 1978	Collection of reports by parents July 1978
1st year	29%	74%	62%
2nd year	16%	61%	72%
3rd year	estimated 10%	73%	77%
4th year	estimated 10%	61%	67%

PLANNING STAGE 2 - OBJECTIVES OF THE PARENTS' EVENING

What behavioural objectives will meet the stated needs?

It is at this point that general aims and goals should give rise to specific objectives. Behavioural objectives which are precise descriptions of observable behaviour have been used and described in connection with curriculum development (Golby et al., 1975), children with learning difficulties (Ainscow and Tweddle, 1977) and management of organisations (James, 1976) etc., to name but a few. For a parents' evening they describe what the parents will be able to do by the end of the evening as a consequence of having attended. The question, 'What do we want the parents to learn as a result of attending the evening?' had to be asked.

Through discussion the authors arrived at the following modest objectives derived from the goal to improve parents' evenings. (Obviously on other occasions or for other schools they might be different.)

1. That more parents attend the evening than on previous occasions.
2. That more parents attend subsequent evenings than on previous occasions.
3. That parents should be able to write down when asked whether their child is making progress or not in most subjects.

4. That parents should meet and talk with the majority of their child's teachers.
5. That parents should indicate when asked, that good school attendance is likely to help their child's progress in school.

PLANNING STAGE 3 - METHOD AND ARRANGEMENTS

What are the optimal methods and arrangements for achieving the objectives?

Aware that the project was an attempt to bring about some change within the school and cognisant of the growing literature concerning change in organisations and the pitfalls that exist, the guidelines by Georgiades and Phillimore (1975) were particularly useful. It was consequently decided that the principal author should attend the January 1978 evening to meet parents and staff. Many staff were interested in any proposals for encouraging more parents to attend. Before the target evening of July 1978 a meeting of all staff involved was held partly in schooltime and continuing after school. This meeting had the following pre-prepared objectives:

(a) to present a paper describing past attendance at parents' evenings and ideas for improvement (circulated in advance).
(b) to list agreed objectives and methods for the forthcoming evening.

These objectives were achieved with many staff offering exciting suggestions. In the knowledge that the experience should be enjoyable and rewarding for all concerned the following arrangements were undertaken:

1. A letter with an easy reading style was posted to parents via responsible pupils inviting them to a parents' evening explaining that:

   (a) end of term reports would not be sent out with pupils but should be collected during the evening or at any time during the day for the week following the evening;
   (b) refreshments and creche would be provided;

69

(c)   there would be a raffle with an attractive prize, the proceeds going to the P.T.A. fund.

2.   There would be one evening for first and second-year pupils and one for third and fourth years with a time, 6-10 p.m., suitable for staff and parents.
3.   Staff were to:

(a)   ask pupils to take home a list of their subjects and teachers so that parents could decide which they wished to see in advance;
(b)   'sell' the parents' evening to their pupils and to point out any good work saying it would be particularly mentioned to their parents. Threatening pupils with adverse comment to parents was to be avoided, since this could cause a child to put his parents off attending.

4.   On the evening staff were:
(a)   to indicate positive achievements of all children;
(b)   to indicate how parents could help at home;
(c)   to check whether any family circumstances had changed that were relevant to the child in school;
(d)   to remind parents of the relevance of good school attendance;
(e)   to end the interview on a positive note. The interview was to be a positive experience to increase the likelihood of parents coming on subsequent occasions.

5.   A questionnaire to parents was to be prepared to check whether certain objectives were achieved and to consult them about the details of the arrangements. It was to be issued, completed and collected during the evening.
6.   An attendance register of parents was kept.

EVALUATION STAGES

Stages 4 and 5 will be examined together at this point and the following questions asked: Stage 4, to what extent were the method and arrangements satisfactory? Stage 5, were the objectives set for the evening achieved?

RESULTS (PART 1)

All of the objectives were achieved except for objective 2 for which evidence from subsequent evenings will need to be collected.

The data were collected via a questionnaire to parents (first and second-year pupils), parents' attendance register, school registers and observation during the evening. 21% of parents attending gave their opinions on the questionnaire. For objective:

1) more parents did attend than on previous occasions (see table 6.1). The increase is of major proportions;
2) no data available yet;
3) the questionnaire asked, 'After talking with the teachers, do you know how your child is progressing in most subjects?' Replies were: Yes 100% No 0%
4) The questionnaire asked, 'How many of your child's teachers have you talked with?' (during the evening)

Per cent of parents	Teachers seen
3	2 or less
31	3 to 5
45	6 to 10
21	more than 10

Most parents (66%) managed to see the majority of their child's teachers.

5) The questionnaire asked, 'Is attending school regularly likely to help your child's progress in school?' Replies: Yes 97% No 0% No reply 3%.

Unless clear objectives had been set in the planning stage, evaluation would have been impossible since the purpose of the parents' evening would have been obscure.

METHOD AND ARRANGEMENTS

1) Times: The questionnaire asked, 'Is the time of the parents' evening convenient? Replies: Yes 80% No 13% No reply 7%
2) Day: The questionnaire asked, 'Is the day (Monday) of

the parents' evening convenient?' Replies: Yes 100% No 0%

3. Refreshments: Observation indicated that these facilities were well used throughout the evening.
4) Creche: Only two children had been placed in the creche all evening, much to the disappointment of the supervising girls. This is a facility that proved unnecessary. Many parents appeared to have young children with them. This did not create a nuisance as they were well controlled.
5) Teachers: The questionnaire asked, 'Would you rather discuss your child's progress with one teacher or most of his/her teachers?' 80% of the replies were to the effect that parents would prefer to talk with most teachers.

CONCLUSION

Not all aspects of the method and arrangements were evaluated. Too much detailed evaluation may have been an unnecessary intrusion into the evening for many parents and teachers. However, omissions include asking teachers their views of the arrangements, asking non-attending parents why they did not, and on what basis they would. No data was collected to indicate whether teachers conducted the interviews in the fashion agreed or 'sold' the idea of parents' evening to the pupils as was planned. There is a limit to what is feasible and desirable but the framework used certainly allows for any of the methods and arrangements to be evaluated, if thought necessary.

The arrangements chosen are but one set of possibilities available, but they did result in the achievement of all the objectives examined so far and their evaluation leaves points to be considered in the planning of subsequent evenings.

RESULTS (PART 2)

More parents did attend the evening than on the previous occasion, but let us consider what other variables are associated with parental attendance. Tables 6.2 and 6.3 summarise the attendances and parental collection of reports for the January and July 1978 evenings. The 'parental collection of reports' figure indicates the total number of reports collected - either during the evening or later in the following week. Focusing on a comparison between attendances in January and July for the first year (Table 6.2) there is an increase of between two and four fold for each class. The remedial class 1 - 3 blue in fact shows the largest increase.

Table 6.2: A comparison of attendance at January and July 1978 Parents' Evenings and parental collection of reports for first-year classes

Per cent Attendance at Parents' Evening

Class	January 1978	July 1978	July 1978 parental collection of reports
1-1	39	93	93
1-2	35	77	96
1-3 blue	13	50	63
1-4 red	28	69	73

Table 6.3: A comparison of atendance at the January and July 1978 Parents' Evenings and parental collection of reports for second-year classes

Per cent Attendance at Parents' Evening

Class	January 1978	July 1978	July 1978 parental collection of reports
2-1	27	72	86
2-2	21	79	86
2-3	16	54	63
2-4	4.5	29	43

For the parents of second-year pupils (Table 6.3) similar increases in attendance are found with the remedial class 2-4 showing the largest increase. This suggests that the organisation of the July 1978 Parents' Evening had a very large effect on parents of remedial children. They can be encouraged to come into school.

Inviting parents to collect reports during the week

following Parents' Evening brought in extra parents who would otherwise not have set foot in the school.

PARENTAL CONTACT WITH SCHOOL AND PUPIL ABILITY

It would appear from Tables 6.2 and 6.3 that parental contact decreases from classes for able to those for less able children. This finding was significant for both years examined (Table 6.4 and 6.5). The results were similar for parental collection of reports.

Table 6.4: Attendance at Parents' Evening July 1978 and pupils stream - 1st year

Class	1-1	1-2	1-3B	1-4R	Total
Parents attended	26	20	12	18	76
Parents not attended	2	6	12	8	28
Total	28	26	24	26	104

chi square = 12.2 for 3 df. $P < .01$ significant

Table 6.5: Attendance at Parents' Evening July 1978 and pupils stream - 2nd year

Class	2-1	2-3	2-3	2-4	Total
Parents attended	21	22	13	6	62
Parents not attended	8	6	11	13	38
Total	29	28	24	19	100

chi square = 12.6 for 3 df. $P < .01$ significant

PARENTAL CONTACT WITH SCHOOL AND PUPIL SCHOOL ATTENDANCE

Both Jones (1976) and Lynch and Pimlot (1976) mention an association between parental contact and pupil school attendance. Tables 6.6 and 6.7 show this to be the case in the present study. For first and second-year pupils, parents who attended the July evening are associated with having children who were good school attenders over the past year. Children were grouped according to their attendance over the previous three terms: Group 1 - attendance 91% or more; Group 2 - 75/90%; Group 3 - less than 75%.

Table 6.6: Parents' attendance at July 1978 evening and pupil school attendance for the past year. First-year pupils

Attendance	Group 1	Group 2	Group 3	Total
Parents attended	46	24	3	73
Parents not attended	13	7	8	28
Total	59	31	11	101

chi square = 12.8 for 2 df. $P<.01$ significant

Table 6.7: Parents' attendance at July 1978 evening and pupil school attendance for the past year. Second-year pupils

Attendance	Group 1	Group 2	Group 3	Total
Parents attended	31	27	3	61
Parents not attended	17	12	9	38
Total	48	39	12	99

chi square = 7.88 for 2 df. $P = .02$ significant

CONCLUSIONS

Parents of able well attending children are most likely to attend, whilst those of remedial poor attending children are least likely to attend, parents' evening. Though the relationship is not proved to be causal encouraging greater home-school contact may improve pupil attendance.

The value of these findings is that they show that differences between parents do exist in terms of pupil variables, but that even though remedial children are less well represented in parental contact with the school, real improvements are possible with this group. Some of the largest increases in contact have been with remedial classes, namely, a five-fold increase for class 1-3b and a ten-fold improvement for class 2-4, comparing parent attendance in January 1978 with that in July 1978.

EVALUATION STAGE 6

Did the Parents' Evening help meet the needs of the school?

Certainly greater home-school contact has been generated, particuarly for remedial children. However, to what extent:

(a) has the understanding by the parents, pupils and staff of the aims of the school been improved?

(b) have the atendance, commitment of pupils and parental cooperation been improved?

Only careful future monitoring of these variables will show the trend of their change, and the extent to which improved parental contact may have contributed.

FINAL COMMENT

Significantly more parents were encouraged to attend the July 1978 Parents' Evening than had attended on previous occasions. Parental attendance and collection of reports have been found to be associated with pupils' level of attainments and school attendance.

Major changes occurred in the proportion of parents of remedial children, who made contact with the school. The most likely measures to have contributed to these changes are having parents collect reports on parents' evening, or during the following week, with letters being posted by responsible pupils, rather than the previous practice of sending end of term reports and parents' evening invitations via the pupils.

Future parents' evenings might have more ambitious objectives involving telling parents what steps their child has achieved and what the next steps of new learning are for each subject. The arrangements might not only ask parents to collect reports at parents' evening, or during the week from school, but also entail form teachers visiting the few parents thus far not contacted, in order to deliver the school report. Such a visit may well be welcomed (Bynner, 1974; Lynch and Pimlot, 1976), but also if positively conducted bring more parents into a closer relationship with school.

Home-school contact might be improved by any of the following arrangements some of which are suggested by

Jones (1976) and Lynch and Pimlot (1976):

1. Develop parent-teacher discussion groups within the P.T.A. to teach parents: (a) about the work of (initially) first-year pupils, (b) how they can help at home, (c) about aspects of education and careers.
2. If the curriculum were organised as a set of target objectives to be achieved by pupils then a booklet, passing between home and school on a monthly basis, could be used to record achievement of these targets. Parents and pupils would be able to see what was achieved and what should be worked on next.
3. Make more school information available to parents via information booklets.
4. Provide more functions at which parents and staff can interact.
5. The P.T.A. could have 'new members' nights when parents rarely seen could be invited by face-to-face invitation from other P.T.A. members visiting them at home.

Although the questionnaire showed that parents wanted to see the majority of their child's teachers on Parents' Evening, some schools do operate a system where parents discuss their child's progress in all subjects with the form teacher who has before him the grades and comments from subject teachers. This system does allow appointments to be made, and could cost parents the time of one interview rather than a whole evening. However, it can be operated only in schools where form teachers actually teach the pupils under their pastoral care.

To do more home-school liaison work, the teachers asked in Lynch and Pimlot's (1976) study, replied that they needed more teachers and more pay to do it. Lynch and Pimlot did not agree, feeling that existing E.W.O.s and school counsellors could be further utilised. A case could be made out for appointing more teachers, to allow more of this sort of work and other aspects of school-based evaluation to be undertaken. It is a possibility that such a policy would assist schools in seeing that many problems including truancy, disruptive behaviour etc., can be better solved or ameliorated by changes inside the school (Carroll, 1977; Mortimore, 1977) than by further proliferation of support services like child guidance centres, E.W.O.s, inspectors and administrative staff (Reynolds and

Murgatroyd, 1977).

However, Lynch and Pimlot do sound a warning note. Both their study and this present one were based on the strategy of action-research; that is an approach which starts from more or less clearly defined policy objectives and attempts to articulate these in terms of a programme of action and research and which will lead to more refined policy and more efficient implementation. The danger is that such research becomes unscientific.

Whatever action is undertaken, it is becoming increasingly clear that parents are a largely untapped potential force in the systematic education of their own children.

REFERENCES

Ainscow, M. and Tweedle, D.A. (1977) 'Behavioural objectives and children with learning difficulties.' Association of Educational Psychologists Journal Volume 4, 5, 33-7

Ainscow, M., Bond, D., Gardner, J. and Twedle, D.A. (1978) 'The development in a three part evaluation procedure for inset course.' British Journal of In-Service Education. Volume 4, 3, 184-90

Bynner, J. (1974) 'Deprived parents.' New Society, 21st February, 448-9

Carroll, H.C.M. (1977) Absenteeism in South Wales. Studies of pupils, their homes and Secondary School. Swansea Faculty of Education. University of Swansea

Dougherty, E.H. and Dougherty, A. (1977) 'The daily report card: A simplified and flexible package for classroom behaviour management.' Psychology in the Schools. Volume 14, 2, 191-5

Fryer, K. (1973) 'Parental involvement scheme: infant and junior.' Remedial Education, Volume 8, 2, 35-6

Georgiades, N.J. and Phillimore, L. (1975) 'The myth of the hero-innovator and alternative strategies for organisational change.' Kiernan, C. and Woodford, F.P. (eds) Behaviour Modification with the Severely Retarded. Amsterdam: Associated Scientific Publishers

Goldby, M., Greenwood, J. and West, R. (1975) Curriculum Development. London: Croom Helm

Gregory, R.P. (1980) 'Planning school-based action research into truancy.' Journal Association of Educational

Psychologists, Volume 5, 3, 30-4
Gregory, R.P. (1981) 'Planning and evaluating a parents' evening in a secondary school.' Comprehensive Education, 42, 24-5
Herbert, G.W. (1976) 'Social problems: identification and action.' Early Identification of Educationally at Risk Children. Wedell, K. and Raybould, E.C., Educational Review No. 6, University of Birmingham
James, R. (1976) 'Management by objectives.' Social Work Today, No. 21, 655-7
Jones, A. (1976) 'The single-parent child in the inner city school.' National Childrens' Bureau Concern No. 20, 20-3
Lynch, J. and Pimlot, J. (1976) Parents and Teachers. Schools Council Research Studies. London: Macmillan Education
Mortimore, P. (1977) 'Schools as institutions.' Educational Research, Volume 20, 1, 61-8
Reynolds, D. and Murgatroyd, S.J. (1977) 'The sociology of schooling and the absent pupil. The school as a factor in the generation of truancy.' In H.C.M. Carroll (ed.), op. cit.
Schools Council (1970) Cross'd with Adversity: the Education of Social Disadvantaged Children in Secondary School working paper 27. Evans: Methuen Educational. London
Stickney, D.M. (1978) 'The fading out of gains in successful compensatory education programmes.' Urban Education, Volume 12, 3, 271-82
Wedge, P. and Prosser, H. (1973) Born to Fail. London: Arrow Books/National Children's Bureau
Wilby, P. (1978) 'The cane: who uses it abroad?' Sunday Times 17th September

Chapter Seven

DISADVANTAGED PARENTS AND CONTACT WITH SECONDARY SCHOOL*

INTRODUCTION

It has long been known that the children of parents interested in their child's education tend to do better at school than those of parents who are not. This has led to increasing interest in the involvement of parents with their child's school. Bynner (1974) found amongst 3,000 parents, that most visited their child's primary school but far fewer working class parents than middle class did so for secondary schooling (40 per cent compared to 80 per cent visiting respectively). Such findings are not uncommon (Lynch and Pimlot, 1976). Particularly at risk are the children of socially disadvantaged families, being more prone to educational failure, delinquency and going into local authority care, than other children (Rutter and Madge, 1976). Cognisant of such findings, attempts were made in the present study to improve parental contact with a secondary school.

PROJECT

The school is mixed, changing from secondary modern to comprehensive three years ago. It is situated in a suburb of the West Midlands, consisting mainly of council housing and very few owner-occupied houses. It has four form intake and approximately 630 pupils. Staff were concerned that

*Reprinted by kind permission from Therapeutic Education, 8, 2, 23-26, 1980

parents' evenings were poorly attended. As a consequence plans were drawn up to try and encourage more parents to attend. Letters were posted to parents by responsible pupils inviting them to collect end-of-term reports at parents' evening or any time during the week before the end of term in July. The previous practice had been that pupils took home their own reports and parents only had parents' evening in which to see teachers.

For further details of the planning and evaluation of the evening see Gregory, Meredith and Woodward (1982).

FINDINGS

A parents' attendance register for the parents' evening and the dinner register provided the source of data. In a similar way to Galloway 1976 receipt of free school meals was taken as the measure of social disadvantage of a family. Such data are very easily available to schools. Approximately 16 per cent of first and second-year pupils received free school meals.

Table 7.1: Attendance at parents' evening and receipt of free school meals: for first and second-year pupils

	Free meals	Not free meals	Total
Parents attended	13	124	137
Parents not attended	19	47	66
Total	32	171	203

chi square = 11.08 for 1 df. P < .0005 significant

Table 7.1 shows that parents who are disadvantaged are significantly less likely to attend parents' evening than non-disadvantaged parents. In fact only approximately 30 per cent did attend.

'Collecting reports' is the sum of those who collected reports either on parents' evening and during the day the following week. It can be seen that offering the latter facility did encourage more of both groups of parents to make contact with the school. 75 per cent and 50 per cent contact for disadvantaged parents of first and second-year pupils is a respectable achievement when compared to

Table 7.2: Attendance at parents' evening and collection of reports by disadvantaged and non-disadvantaged parents of first-year pupils

	Disadvantaged Parents		Non-disadvantaged Parents		Total	
Attended parents' evening	8/16	50%	68/88	77%	76/104	74%
Collected reports	12/16	75%	73/88	83%	85/104	82%

Table 7.3: Attendance at parents' evening and collection of reports by disadvantaged and non-disadvantaged parents of second-year pupils

	Disadvantaged Parents		Non-disadvantaged Parents		Total	
Attended parents' evening	5/16	31%	56/83	67%	61/99	61%
Collected reports	8/16	50%	65/83	78%	73/99	72%

Table 7.4: The percentage extra parental contact brought about by offering the facility to collect reports during the day for the week after parents' evening. (For first and second-year pupils.)

	Parents of 1st-year pupils		Parents of 2nd-year pupils		Total	
Disadvantaged parents	4/16	25%	3/16	19%	7/32	22%
Non-disadvantaged parents	5/88	6%	9/83	11%	14/171	8%
Total	9/104	8%	12/99	11%		

Bynner's findings that only 40 per cent of parents of social class IV and V make contact.

But it is Table 7.4 that shows that nearly three times more disadvantaged parents made use of the day-time facility compared to other parents (22 per cent compared to

8 per cent).

CONCLUSION

Parents' evening on this occasion militated against the disadvantaged, whereas the day-time facility greatly encouraged contact with such parents. A large proportion of them did have contact with the school (Tables 7.2 and 7.3) and thus it may not necessarily be true that disadvantaged parents are not in contact with school because they are uninterested in their child's education. A search for other reasons should be made and a starting point may be the interaction between the school's organisation of home-school contacts and the environmental sanctions against such parents taking-up such arrangements. For example 60 per cent of the parents of second-year pupils came from one-parent or large families; five or more children (Gregory, 1983). Shift work and finding baby sitters may make visiting school in the evening a problem for some families.

Care should be taken in generalising these results too far but they raise the need for other schools to look critically at the efficiency of their home-school contact arrangements.

SUMMARY

Attempts were made at a secondary school in the West Midlands, to improve parental contact between home and school. The findings indicate that the parents' evening militated against the attendance of disadvantaged parents, but that an invitation to visit school during the day to collect their child's report and discuss with staff was taken up by proportionally more disadvantaged parents than others.

It may be that such parents are known to have poor contact with school not because of their lack of interest in education but because of their difficulties in taking advantage of the home-school contact arrangements made by school.

There is a need for more school-based evaluation in this area.

REFERENCES

Bynner, J. (1974) 'Deprived parents.' New Society, 21st February, 448-9

Galloway, D.M. (1976) 'Size of school-socioeconomic hardship suspension rates and persistent unjustified absence from school.' British Journal of Educational Psychology, 46, 1, 40-7

Gregory, R.P. (1983) 'Examining a secondary school's withdrawal system of help for pupils with remedial problems. An example of within-school evaluation.' Journal of Applied Educational Studies, 12, 1, 44-55

Gregory, R.P., Meredith, P. and Woodward, A. (1982) 'Parental Involvement in Secondary School.' Journal of the Association of Educational Psychologists, 5, 8, 54-60

Lynch, J. and Pimlot, J. (1976) Parents and teachers. Schools Council Research Studies. London: Macmillan Educational

Rutter, M. and Madge, N. (1976) Cycles of Disadvantage. London: Heinemann

Chapter Eight

CORRECTIVE READING PROGRAMME: THE USE OF
EDUCATIONAL TECHNOLOGY IN A SECONDARY
SCHOOL*

R.P. Gregory, C. Hackney and N.M. Gregory

The existence of many secondary school remedial
departments bears witness to the numerous children who by
secondary age have not yet mastered, for various reasons,
the skill of reading. That some children can still be taught
to read at this late stage is supported by the good records of
many remedial departments. The problem is to bring about
swift reading gains in the least possible time.

The present study endeavoured to compare the reading
gains of first-year secondary aged children using their
current remedial reading programme, with the gains
produced using the Corrective Reading Programme
published by Science Research Associates (SRA).

Corrective reading was developed on the basis of direct
instructional principles. The most well known are the nine
DISTAR programmes published by SRA. The letters stand
for 'direct instructional systems for teaching and
remediation'. There are three programmes in reading,
arithmetic and language.

These programmes are but an example of the increasing
use of what can be called educational technology or
instructional materials designed on the basis of behavioural
objectives and systems theory.

Specifically the DISTAR programmes and Corrective
Reading were designed on the basis of principles described
in great detail by Becker and Engelmann (1976) and Becker
et al. (1975a, b).

However not only can behavioural objectives be used to

*Reprinted with kind permission from School Psychology
International, 2, 2, 21-5, 1981

design reading language and mathematics programmes but also wider curriculum activities for slow learners (Ainscow and Tweddle, 1979) and also for students following a secondary school curriculum (Briggs, 1970; Gagne and Briggs, 1974).

Such programmes of objectives could be worked out for any secondary school subject, e.g. science, history, french, geography, etc.

The major advantage of writing programmes in these terms is that one specifies what the student should be able to do as a result of having been taught a set of lessons. So instead of, for example, in geography just describing the teaching goal of 'teach the British Isles', this would become a sequence of objectives from easy to more difficult steps ending in, for example, the student being able to:

> write down a list of the major regions of the British Isles and describe the major industries in each.

It may be that having taught to the same goal you would expect much less from students in the lowest forms, namely having a final objective more like:

> having been taught the course on the British Isles, students should be able to write down:
>
> (a)   the countries making up the British Isles
> (b)   ten counties of England
> (c)   ten major cities and mark them approximately on a map provided
> (d)   five major rivers and mark them approximately on a map provided, etc.

Such specification allows one to give students a list of the objectives to be mastered in a given subject and for them to record their own progress by marking off those achieved. As with Corrective Reading a points system could be used as an extra motivational tool. Points would be awarded for the successful completion of work. These could be totalled and cashed in for the schools' housepoints. Some schools have special ceremonies for awarding certificates when children gain ten housepoints in school.

TRIAL BASIS

Task-analysed programmes of objectives have a great deal to offer a secondary school and especially the remedial department, since it might be conceived as the remedial teacher's role to help other subject departments to write such programmes for the less academic pupils coming under the auspices of the remedial department. As a step in that direction the present authors examined the possibility of using a commercially available programme - Corrective Reading - and using it on a trial basis. Interest was such that a teacher in the school's French Department offered to teach level A of the programme (not described here) whilst the second author taught level B.

Children aged eleven through to school leaving age who have made a start with reading but who are still at a remedial level are the target of Corrective Reading. The programme aims at group teaching and not individualised instruction. It consists of three levels - Decoding A, B and C:

Decoding A is the simplest level (60 lessons);
Decoding B teaches work-attack skills and comprehension (140 lessons);
Decoding C teaches skill application (140 lessons).

One lesson should be taught each day with a group of children ranging up to a maximum of 15. The teacher has to follow a script which initially can appear tedious but soon becomes a vehicle for the teacher's own creativity in teaching and child management. A points system for reading achievement is an integral part of the programme.

Thorne (1978) used Corrective Reading Decoding B with junior aged children at a residential school for the maladjusted. The children ranged in age from seven to thirteen. On average the group gained six months in reading accuracy and comprehension (on the Neal Analysis of Reading Ability) in seven weeks of teaching (one lesson per day).

Another study in Australia by Maggs and Murdoch (1979) used the programme with upper primary and early secondary aged pupils with marked reading deficits. The primary children showed ten months and twelve months gain in comprehension and reading accuracy respectively in seven months of teaching. With the more severely affected secondary pupils gains of 25 months and eleven months were achieved for comprehension and reading accuracy, again in seven months of teaching. Both of these studies used contracts and awarded points for reading achievement.

THE PROJECT

The present project was undertaken in a comprehensive school for some 600 pupils and four form entry. The intake comes largely from a nearby council housing estate. For the first three years the forms are organised into a top, middle and two parallel remedial forms. Pupils with reading ages of nine years or less on the Daniels and Diack Test of Reading Experience are given extra tuition by the remedial teacher. From the two parallel remedial classes 1-3 and 1-4, eleven children were chosen using matched pairs, as far as possible, for the Corrective Reading placement test, reading age, age and social disadvantage, to make up the group to be taught using Corrective Reading B. For organisational reasons all of these children were from class 1-3. Their average age was 11 years 9 months. Eight children made up the group who were to be taught on the school's current remedial programme, and were all from class 1-4. They were the comparison group, the average age being 11 years 10 months.

The two groups were broadly comparable in pretest reading age, average error rate and starting point (placement) on the Corrective Reading placement test (B1 means the child should start Corrective Reading Level B at lesson one - see Tables 8.2 and 8.3). It was therefore assumed that the intelligence or aptitude for learning reading for the two groups was also comparable. However no intelligence test was administered.

The experimental group was made up of four boys and seven girls. The comparison group consisted of six boys and two girls. The two groups were obviously not comparable in this respect.

Support from home can be a vital factor in a child's reading progress (Wilby, 1981). Since such support is correlated in this respect with the social class of parents, the extent of social disadvantage (as measured by receipt of free school meals) in the two groups was investigated and found to be comparable with 36 per cent disadvantaged in the experimental group and 38 per cent in the comparison group.

The teacher of the Corrective Reading group also taught the comparison group for half of their remedial periods. Both teachers had taught in secondary schools for similar lengths of time but the experimental group teacher was much more experienced in teaching remedial children. This teacher was trained in the use of Corrective Reading. The comparison group teacher was not taught how to use the school's current remedial materials but just given advice in their use.

The school's current remedial programme consisted of the use of:

(a)   SRA reading laboratory 1c and 2a;
(b)   Blackwell Spelling workshop
(c)   Wolverhampton Supply Company phonic programme;
(d)   Blackwell Talk, Write and Spell;
(e)   Handwriting practice;
(f)   General language work (spoken and written).

Parts of the above were used, as and when considered appropriate, to teach the comparison group. No strict pattern of use was maintained. Much of this material allows for individualised instruction and is different from the group instruction of Corrective Reading.

Continuity between the work of both teachers was maintained to a degree. Much of the material used is sequential allowing the teacher to know on which work-card a child is working. The pupils just continued with the work with one teacher from where they left off with the other. The handwriting practice and general language work has less continuity as detailed discussions between the teachers on what had been taught and what should come next, were not held.

GROUP TESTING

All pupils were tested on Daniels and Diack Test of Reading Experience in January 1980 and again in June. Group testing on both occasions was completed by the second author. The fact that this testing was not done by an independent tester and that this teacher knew whether the students were in the experimental or comparison groups (the testing was not blind) is a failing that could not be overcome. Such

Table 8.1: Gains in reading ages for past groups of children with reading difficulties, from the first year to third year, receiving the school's current remedial programme

Group	Mean REA yrs		Mean REA yrs July 1979	Mean gain in years in reading age in 12 months
First year (n = 30) (23 boys; 7 girls)	7.4	Sept 1978	8.2	0.96
Second year (n = 14) (9 boys; 5 girls)	8.0	July 1978	8.9	0.96
Third year (n = 11) (9 boys; 2 girls)	7.0	July 1978	8.0	1.0

Note: REA = Daniels and Diack graded reading experience age.

problems are well known to action-researchers working in the natural environment.

The Corrective Reading group received lessons on Monday, period three, Thursday, periods three and seven and Friday, period four. The comparison group received lessons on Monday, periods three and six, Thursday, period four and Friday, period six. Period six was just before dinner time. It was assumed that the pattern of teaching periods would not create differences between the groups.

The experimental group teacher was monitored by the psychologist and the second teacher for the comparison group was monitored by the experimental group teacher, ensuring that both programmes were taught correctly. Even though the inexperienced comparison group teacher only received advice on the use of the school's current remedial materials, she used them appropriately according to the experimental teacher's observations.

One difference between the two groups was the degree of support received from the psychologist. This had been extensive for the experimental group teacher but nil for that of the comparison group. This difference is obviously likely to contribute to differences in the reading gains between the groups. The time spent on teaching the Corrective Reading programme was exactly equal to that received by the comparison group. Fortunately the Corrective Reading materials were bought for the school by the remedial adviser of the local authority on condition that a report of the experiment was produced. Other remedial services of local education authorities have bought the materials and loaned them to schools on a semi-permanent basis. This avoids a school wasting money on a scheme that may not suit them, but also allows the service which owns the kit to have some control over the competence with which it is taught. The kit can always be withdrawn.

RESULTS

Table 8.1 presents the gains in reading of past remedial groups in this school using the equipment mentioned above and taught by the experimental group teacher. Gains are of the order of one year of reading age and achieved in one year of teaching.

In Table 8.2 one can see the results for the comparison group. On average they made 0.2 years or approximately

Table 8.2: Comparison group – using the school's current remedial materials

Subjects
6 boys, 2 girls (N = 8) from class 1-4

Socially disadvantaged
38 per cent

Teachers
2 periods with the experimental group teacher and 2 periods with a second teacher (not experienced in remedial work) and not specifically trained but only given advice in the use of the school's current remedial materials.

Materials
Largely commercially available kits of individualised work.

Support from psychologist
Nil

Time spent on the programme
4 periods per week for 5 months

Testing
The Daniels and Diack test of reading experience (a group test) was administered by the second author. This was not done blind i.e. he was aware of whether the children were experimental or comparison. The Corrective Reading placement test was administered by the first author.

Results: pre- and post-test reading ages

| Subjects | Age Jan 1980 | Sex | Corrective Reading Placement Test | | Reading ages REA | | |
			Errors on Part 1	Placement	Jan 1980 Pre-test	June 1980 Post-test	Gain in years
1	12-3	M	19	B1	7.8	7.1	-0.7
2	11-7	F	24	B1	7.4	7.6	0.2
3	11-8	M	13	B1	8.8	9.0	0.2
4	11-11	M	10	B61	8.3	8.2	-0.1
5	12-3	F	11	B1	7.0	7.6	0.6
6	11-11	M	20	B1	7.1	7.4	0.3
7	11-5	M	17	B1	7.6	7.8	0.2
8	11-9	M	5	C1	8.8	10.0	1.2
Mean	11-10		14.9		7.85	8.08	0.23
Mean Boys (6)	11-10		14.0		8.07	8.25	0.18
Mean Girls (2)	11-11		17.5		7.20	7.60	0.40

REA = Daniels and Diack graded reading experience age

Table 8.3: Experimental group - using Corrective Reading

Subjects
4 boys, 7 girls (N = 11) from class 1-3

Socially disadvantaged
36 per cent

Teacher
Experienced in remedial work, trained to use Corrective Reading.

Materials
Corrective Reading teacher and student books for group teaching.

Support from psychologist
20 meetings over 17 months

Time spent on the programme
4 periods per week for 5 months

Testing
The Daniels and Diack test of reading experience, a group test, was administered by the second author. This was not done blind i.e. he was aware of whether the children were experimental or comparison. The Corrective Reading placement test was administered by the first author.

Corrective Reading
Placement Test | Reading ages REA

Subjects	Age Jan 1980	Sex	Errors on Part I	Place- ment	Jan 1980 Pre-test	June 1980 Post-test	Gain in years	Corrective Reading Number of lessons completed
1	12-3	M	15	B1	7.7	9.1	1.4	57
2	11-8	F	8	B1	8.4	11.2	2.8	55
3	11-4	M	15	B1	8.3	10.3	2.0	55
4	12-0	F	35	B1	8.6	9.5	0.9	57
5	11-7	F	21	B1	7.9	10.0	2.1	55
6	11-10	M	11	B61	8.4	10.0	1.6	53
7	11-11	M	17	B1	8.4	11.2	2.8	53
8	11-5	F	4	C1	8.6	10.0	1.4	57
9	11-9	F	10	B1	8.1	9.3	1.2	44
10	11-10	F	-	C1	8.6	9.7	1.1	55
11	11-5	F			8.7	10.3	1.6	56
Mean	11-9		16.9		8.3	10.1	1.8	
Mean Boys (4)	11-10		18.5		8.2	10.15	1.95	
Mean Girls (7)	11-6		15.8		8.4	10.0	1.60	

REA = Daniels and Diack graded reaching experience age

two months' progress in five months' of teaching. Not only is this a fraction of the progress of the Corrective Reading group, it is half that of past remedial groups using this reading equipment. It may be that having two teachers rather than one has something to do with these low gains.

Table 8.3 presents the pre- and post-test reading ages for the Corrective Reading group. It can be seen that on average 1.8 years in reading age was achieved in five months of teaching. Some individual pupils were making nearly three years' progress in that time. The group reached lesson 26 of Corrective Reading. Thus they were taking two periods to complete one lesson. Interestingly the boys (n = 4) made on average gains of 1.95 years whilst the girls (n = 7) on average gained 1.60 years. It is not immediately clear why the boys should do better than the girls, since the girls start with a better average error rate on the placement test and a higher average pre-test reading age.

However, for whatever reason, the Corrective Reading group shows astonishing progress. One can tentatively attribute this difference to the difference in reading programmes, since the two groups were comparable except for (i) the sex distribution (ii) the comparison group having two teachers and one of these being inexperienced in remedial work and (iii) support from the psychologist.

DISCUSSION

The results of this study, with those of Maggs and Murdoch (1979) and Thorne (1978), indicate that it is within the bounds of possibility for a secondary school to practically eliminate remedial reading problems across the first year of secondary schooling. The slowest child made gains of approximately a year in the study in five months. Remember that only part of the Corrective Reading programme was completed. Undoubtedly some progress of the pupils was due, in part, to the fact that they were an experimental group and being taught by an enthusiastic teacher. Possibly the gains will be less spectacular in the following year. However, it demonstrates that such reading gains can be achieved for whatever reason. This puts such pupils in a better position to take advantage of the English-based subjects like history, geography and religious education. The teachers of these subjects will no longer have to struggle to teach their subject and remedial reading to the weakest children. Nevertheless, the time the teacher must initially spend in learning Corrective Reading could be a problem. One must practice with another member of staff and other pupils before commencing teaching. Hearing all pupils read was a problem overcome by doing it in lesson time, but a more suitable possibility to explore might be, in view of the results of parental involvement in the reading of socially disadvantaged children described by Wilby (1981), to allow the students to take their student books home and have their parents hear them read. This could be preceded by calling a meeting of these parents to explain 'do's and dont's' of the task. Also points gained could be cashed in for rewards at home. That these parents might welcome such an activity is supported by work previously carried out at this school (Gregory, 1980; Gregory et al., 1982).

Timetabling arrangements, to have one teacher with a small group of children (eight to 15 pupils) was a difficult issue. But if the gains described here can be maintained for further teaching time and are reproducible in other secondary schools, the advantages would appear to be greatly worth the inconvenience of having to timetable around the Corrective Reading groups required. Such developments obviously require forward planning by the school.

There has been no shortage of enthusiasm on the part of the other staff in the school. Already a member of the history department has commenced some teaching of Corrective Reading for a second phase of the experiment. He greatly enjoys the structure the material gives to the curriculum content and to his classroom management. He has welcomed the feedback given by the psychologist in his role of programme monitor in which he collects observational data during a Corrective Reading lesson, to ensure the programme is being taught appropriately. The observational data includes pupil response rates, frequency of teacher praise and reprimand, frequency with which the teacher gains pupils' attention before teaching a task, etc. In short there is the facility to check teacher competence.

With the success of this trial use of a commercially available hierarchically task-analysed programme of objectives, impetus is given to the endeavour of production of such programmes for the less able pupils in the school for subjects like geography, history, etc. Not only might these programmes bring the advantages described earlier but also engender the desire to evaluate as carefully as possible the effects of such programmes, and hence bring the concept of evaluation as a routine event, to many more teachers.

NOTE

R.P. Gregory is a psychologist with the Birmingham Child Guidance and Psychological Service, C. Hackney is Head of the Remedial Department at Paget Secondary School, Birmingham, and N.M. Gregory is Head of the Mathematics Department at Cardinal Wiseman R.C. Secondary School, Birmingham.

BIBLIOGRAPHY

Ainscow, M. and Tweddle, D.A. (1979) Preventing Classroom Failure: An Objective Approach. New York: Wiley

Becker, W.C. and Engelmann, S. (1976) Teaching 3 Evaluation of Instruction. Chicago: Science Research Associates

Becker, W.C., Engelmann, S. and Thomas, D.R. (1975a) Teaching 1 Classroom Management. Chicago: Science Research Associates

Becker, W.C., Engelmann, S. and Thomas, D.R. (1975b) Teaching 2 Cognitive Learning and Instruction. Chicago: Science Research Associates

Briggs, L.J. (1970) Handbook of Procedures for the Design of Instruction. Washington D.C.: American Institutes for Research

Gagne, R.M. and Briggs, L.J. (1974) Principles of Instructional Design. London: Holt, Rinehart Winston

Gregory, R.P. (1980) 'Disadvantaged parents and contact with secondary school.' Therapeutic Education. 8(2), 23-6

Gregory, R.P., Meredith, P.T. and Woodward, A.J. (1982) 'Parental involvement in a secondary school.' Journal of the Association of Educational Psychologists, 5, 8, 54-60

Maggs, A. and Murdoch, R. (1979) 'Teaching low performance in upper primary and lower secondary to read by direct instructional methods.' Reading Education, September

Thorne, T. (1978) 'Payment for reading. The use of the 'Corrective Reading Scheme' with junior maladjusted

boys.' Remedial Education 13(2), 87-90
Wilby, P. (1981) 'The Belfield experiment.' Sunday Times
Weekly Review March

Chapter Nine

CORRECTIVE READING PROGRAMME: AN EVALUATION*

R.P. Gregory, C. Hackney and N.M. Gregory

SUMMARY

The four purposes of this paper were: (a) to provide further evaluative data on the Corrective Reading programme; (b) to carry out action-research with the aim of organisational change in the host secondary school; (c) to demonstrate within-school evaluation; and (d) to experiment with an alternative role to that of casework for an educational psychologist.

Some of the Direct Instruction and the Corrective Reading programme literature was reviewed. A model of evaluation incorporating a planned-change model of innovation provides the framework of the paper. The Corrective Reading programme was used with an experimental group of first-year secondary-aged children (N = 11) with reading problems, and compared with the school's own remedial provision with a comparison group of similar children (N = 8). In 5 months of teaching the experimental group, on average, gained 1.8 years in reading whilst the comparison group gained 0.2 years. The experimental group also maintained good school behaviour and improved attendance, more so than the comparison group.

This paper exemplifies the co-operation between psychologist and school in evaluating current and proposed new practice. Such a role for a psychologist is likely to generate more organisational definitions and solutions of school problems than is usual in casework.

*Reprinted with kind permission from the British Journal of Educational Psychology, 52, 33-50, 1982

Corrective Reading Programme: An Evaluation

INTRODUCTION

This paper has four main purposes to fulfil. Firstly, it is an attempt to provide further evaluative data concerning the effectiveness of the Corrective Reading programme (published by Science Research Associates) with secondary-aged children with reading problems. There has been little evaluation of this programme other than Thorne (1978) and Maggs and Murdoch (1979), although the principles of direct instruction on which it is based have undergone extensive evaluation (Gordon, 1971; Becker, 1977; Maggs and Maggs, 1979; Becker et al., 1981).

Secondly, it is action-research aimed at bringing about organisational change in the host school. The objective was the implementation of Corrective Reading with appropriate groups of children as an on-going educational provision, assuming data accumulated during the project made this justifiable. An alternative method (to that used) of changing the organisation of this school's remedial work could have been attempted. However, Georgiades and Phillimore (1975) found little change in an organisation as a consequence of its receiving new information from the hero-innovator-type expert consultant from outside. Katz and Kahn (1978) found little lasting change in workers' behaviour on-site after training off-site. Training courses alone cannot bring about organisational change in an institution (Glen, 1975; Katz and Kahn, 1978). Topping (1977) reviews the efficacy of consultation with an outside consultant as a model of organisational change and finds the results equivocal.

In the light of these findings, particular note was made of work by Stufflebeam et al. (1971), Margulies and Wallace (1973), Georgiades and Phillimore (1975) and Arends and Arends (1977).

The third purpose of this research was to conduct, and in so doing help a school to conduct within-school evaluation. Educational research has principally been involved in searching for principles generalisable across education. Tizard (1976) indicates that there has been little evaluation of actual practice and little within-school evaluation, whilst Stufflebeam et al. (1971), Morrish (1976), Sutton (1977) and Gregory (1980a) argue for more such evaluation.

Morrish (1976) says that many decisions on the implementation of curriculum innovations are currently made on insufficient evidence, a finding supported by Munro

(1977). Stufflebeam et al. (1971) note that it is rare to see the appointment of an evaluator on the staff of a school in the USA.

Fourthly, this paper demonstrates the operation of a role alternative to the traditional one for an educational psychologist. Within-school evaluation could be undertaken by local authority educational psychologists in conjunction with schools willing to critically examine their own practices.

Direct instruction

Corrective Reading was developed on the basis of direct instructional principles. The most well-known programmes are the nine DISTAR programmes published by Science Research Associates (SRA). The letters stand for 'direct instructional systems for teaching and remediation'. There are three programmes in reading, arithmetic and language. Another less well-known programme is 'Corrective Spelling through Morphographs'.

Direct instruction had its origins in the Bereiter-Engelmann pre-school at the University of Illinois in the 1960s and became fully developed under the Follow-through programme which commenced after Headstart.

The DISTAR programmes were designed for use with children aged 5 to 9 in normal school in the USA. Evidence indicates that DISTAR was the most successful of 22 programmes in project Follow-through (Becker, 1977). Project Follow-through has been described as the longest and most expensive social experiment ever launched. It eventually came to involve 180 communities, 75,000 children and an annual budget of 59 million dollars for 9 years.

Behavioural principles and the logical analysis of the development of concepts and operations are the two components constituting direct instruction (Maggs and Murdoch, 1979). Studies using direct instruction have been carried out with retarded children (as low as severely retarded), autistic, non-English speaking, bilingual, deaf, disadvantaged and normal children in all parts of the United States, Canada, Australia and the Pacific Islands (Becker et al., 1981).

Corrective reading

This programme was devised by the authors of DISTAR using the same principles but for children aged 11 through to adults, who have made a start with reading but who are at a remedial level. This programme aims at group teaching, not individualised instruction. It consists of three levels: Decoding A, B and C:

Decoding A   is the simplest level and has 60 lessons;
Decoding B   teaches word attack skills and comprehension (140 lessons);
Decoding C   teaches skill application (140 lessons).

One lesson should be taught each day with a group of children ranging up to 15. The teacher's behaviour is described and scripted. Maggs and Murdoch (1979) used the programme with a withdrawal group of 14 upper primary and early secondary students with marked reading deficits. The primary students made an average gain of 10 months in reading comprehension and 12 months in reading accuracy in 7 months of instruction. With the more severely reading deficient secondary students, gains of 25 months in reading comprehension and 11 months in reading accuracy in 7 months of teaching occurred (Neale Analysis of Reading Ability Tests).

Thorne (1978) used the programme with junior-aged boys ranging in age from 7 to 13 at a residential school for the maladjusted. On average the group gained 6 months in reading accuracy and comprehension in 7 weeks of teaching (one lesson per day).

Neither of these two studies used control or comparison groups but both did make use of contingency contracting and the earning of points.

METHOD

A model of evaluation

This brings us to consideration of the model of evaluation to be used here. That described by Ainscow et al. (1978) and utilised by Gregory (1980a, 1981a) and Gregory et al. (1982) constituted the evaluation framework.

The remainder of this paper will be described within the

context of this model.

Figure 9.1: A model of evaluation

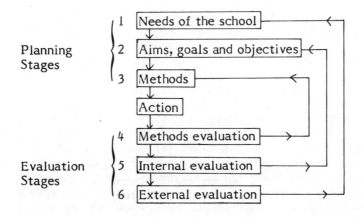

Needs of the school (Stage 1)

The present project followed on from work previously carried out with the school (Gregory, 1980a, 1980b, 1981a, 1982, 1983; Gregory et al., 1982). It became comprehensive from secondary modern some years ago, having approximately 600 pupils and four form intake. The intake comes largely from a council estate with relatively few children from owner-occupied houses. The forms in the first 3 years are organised into a top (1-1), middle (1-2) and two parallel remedial forms (1-3 and 1-4) indicating that the school has a large proportion of children with reading difficulties. Pupils with a reading age of 9 years or less (on Daniels and Diack Test of Reading Experience - Daniels and

Diack, 1972) are withdrawn for extra help with reading from the remedial teacher. Earlier work at the school found that the pupil intake included many socially disadvantaged children who had gross reading difficulties and poor attendance (Gregory, 1983). The findings in Table 9.1 support the view that the school needs a teaching programme to accelerate the reading progress of many children as fast as possible. Table 9.1 shows that in previous years children with reading problems, whether they were first, second or third years, on average gained approximately 1 year in reading age in 12 months using the school's current remedial reading equipment and being taught by the experimental group teacher.

Aims, goals and objectives (Stage 2)

The general aim was to find a way of improving reading standards in the school. The goal derived from this was to attempt to improve the reading of a particular group of first-year pupils. This led to the following sequence of objectives being set for the present study. To simplify matters the specific methods used to achieve each objective are described as well, though technically they should be described under Stage 3.

The general strategy used was the planned-change model of decision making (Stufflebeam et al., 1971, p.72). This planned-change model consists of 11 major steps, five of which (research invention, design construction and assembly) were not relevant to this project because the evaluation was of a commercially available instructional programme. However the following six objectives - dissemination, demonstration, training, trial, installation and institutionalisation - were relevant and are described with the method used to implement them.

Dissemination

The object of this was to inform potential users of the programme's existence and its potential effectiveness. The method used was discussion with the remedial teacher and SRA representative centred on the Corrective Reading Sampler (an advertising pack available from SRA) and articles about the effectiveness of DISTAR and Corrective

Table 9.1: Gains in reading ages for past groups of children with reading difficulties from the first year to third year, receiving the school's current remedial programme

Group	Mean REA yrs		Mean REA yrs July 1979	Mean gain in yrs in reading age in 12 months	SD
First year (N = 30) 23 boys 7 girls	7.4	Sept. 1978	8.2	0.96	0.86
Second year (N = 14) 9 boys 5 girls	8.0	July 1978	8.9	0.9	0.9
Third year (N = 11) 9 boys 2 girls	7.0	July 1978	8.0	1.0	0.87

Note: REA = Daniels and Diack graded reading experience age

Reading, namely Becker (1977), Thorne (1978) and Maggs and Murdoch (1979).

Demonstration

This step afforded an opportunity for the teacher to examine and assess operating qualities of the programme in order to build conviction. Consequently for the method a trainer from SRA put on a demonstration lesson at the school with the experimental group, for the benefit of remedial and English department staff and the deputy head. Afterwards there was an opportunity to discuss operating problems.

Training

The intention was to train a teacher to manage and operate the programme as it is intended to be used. After the demonstration lesson, the programme materials were purchased and the teacher practised first with another member of staff and then later with groups of children. This method is not quite the same as the 'model lead and test' sequence used in project Follow-through (Becker, 1977). The comparison group teacher was not taught how to use the current remedial materials but just given advice on its use.

Trial

The intention here was to build familiarity with the programme and provide a basis for assessing its quality, value and utility in this particular school setting. The use of Corrective Reading was undertaken from the outset as a trial to evaluate its effectiveness in terms of reading gains compared with the comparison group using the school's current remedial equipment. The Corrective Reading materials were bought for the school by the local education authority (LEA) remedial adviser, on condition that a report of the experiment was made available. Other LEA remedial services have loaned DISTAR and Corrective Reading materials to schools, on a semi-permanent basis. This avoids a school wasting money on unsuitable material, but also allows the service to have some control over the competence with which it is taught. The material can always be withdrawn.

The method was to prepare an evaluation design. This had pre- and post-tests of reading, behaviour and attendance for an experimental and comparison group of first-year pupils. The analysis of the data was done using the analysis of covariance (McNemar, 1962).

From the two parallel remedial classes 1-3 and 1-4, 11 children (four boys and seven girls) were chosen using matched pairs as far as was possible for the Corrective Reading placement test, Daniels and Diack reading age, chronological age and social disadvantage, to make up the group to be taught using Corrective Reading level B. For organisational reasons all of these children were from class 1-3. They were withdrawn from the class for this teaching.

Eight children (six boys and two girls) made up the group which was to be taught the school's current remedial programme. They were the comparison group and were all withdrawn from class 1-4.

The experimental group received points for good progress and behaviour during the Corrective Reading periods. The comparison group did remedial work with one of two possible teachers (one of whom was the teacher of the experimental group). They constitute similar groups rather than identical, hence their being a comparison rather than control group (Fitz-Gibbon and Lyons-Morris, 1978).

One reason for having a comparison group was the problem of regression towards the mean. This problem can affect the evaluation of a programme. They can falsely appear to be successful simply because regression has occurred. For this reason, at least, it is important to have a comparison group of some kind, when evaluating remedial programmes. It is important that this control or comparison group has a similar home background to the experimental group because low-scoring students from generally high-achieving groups can be expected to regress more towards the mean on post-test than students from disadvantaged homes. Using a comparison group overcomes some of the problems since both experimental and comparison groups will show regression. Maggs et al. (undated) quote the use of gain scores, group means and standard deviations corrected for regression to the mean, using Mehrens and Lehmann's (1973) procedure.

In an effort to combine this evaluative design with what is called illuminative evaluation (Munro, 1977; Parlett and

Hamilton, 1978), two questions of Corrective Reading programme were asked (Gagne and Briggs, 1974):

(1) In what ways and to what extent is the programme better than what was done before?
(2) What additional, possibly unanticipated, effects has the programme had and to what extent are these better or worse than the previous way things were done?

For this question the following supplementary questions can be asked:

(a) What practical difficulties were encountered in conducting the programme, i.e., timetabling, running over lesson time, checking, marking or costs, etc?
(b) How interested were the pupils in the programme material?
(c) Has the programme had an effect on the behaviour of the pupils in other lessons and their school attendance?
(d) Have staff unconnected with the project commented at all?

An evaluation to answer these questions must concern itself with input, process and outcome variables and measures. To conclude that the difference in reading ages between the experimental group and comparison group was due to the Corrective Reading in the prevailing conditions of this school, one must be sure that the following variables are taken into account for the two groups. The following input variables were considered.

1.   Vision and hearing. Neither group had pupils with untreated vision or hearing problems.
2.   Age and sex. The experimental group of average age 11 : 9 years consisted of four boys and seven girls. The comparison group of average age 11 : 10 years consisted of six boys and two girls. The two groups were obviously not comparable in sex distribution.
3.   The initial level of reading, behaviour and attendance. The initial reading level was measured by the second author prior to the commencement of the project in January 1980, using the Daniels and Diack test of reading experience, a group test (Daniels and Diack, 1972) and again tested in June 1980. This test was used firstly because it had been extensively used in monitoring the reading gains of

past year groups. This provided supplementary comparison data. Secondly, it was used because it was familiar to the teacher. The test demands skills in decoding reading and language comprehension. Reading ages over 10 years are described as unreliable by the test's authors although no reliability figures appear to be published. Although the test is normative, it is testing similar skills to those Corrective Reading Level B purports to teach, namely word attack and reading comprehension skills. Had the choice of test been possible an alternative would have been considered which quoted reliability figures. The fact that the testing was not done by an independent tester and that the tester knew whether the students were in the experimental or comparison groups (the testing was not blind) is a failing that, although appreciated, could not be overcome. Since a group test was used it was felt the opportunity for tester-bias to occur was minimal.

The two groups were broadly comparable in average Corrective Reading placement test error rates, placement, pre-test reading ages and chronological ages. (A placement of B1 means the student should start Corrective Reading level B at lesson one - see Tables 9.2 and 9.3.)

It was therefore assumed that the intelligence or aptitude for learning reading for the two groups was comparable. However, no intelligence testing was administered.

The teachers of Maths and English (as teachers seeing pupils most often) for both groups were given Rutter's children's behaviour questionnaire (Rutter, 1967) before Corrective Reading commenced. It was completed again in June 1980.

Attendances for the three terms were collected for both groups. Term one was the pre-test rate whilst the second and third terms constituted the post-test rate.

Behaviour and attendance were investigated because Rutter et al. (1979) point to a connection between these two variables on the one hand and curriculum planning, teaching style and pupil success on the other. Not only were Rutter's schools different in the extent to which they promoted good attendance and classroom behaviour in their pupils, but these differences were thought to be associated with better group-planning of the syllabus, lesson preparation and class management in the schools showing good results. Good pupil behaviour was found to be strongly associated with the teachers' use of ample praise in their teaching, and their focus on good rather than disruptive behaviour. On the other hand, high levels of punishment were generally associated with worse behaviour, attendance, academic work and delinquency outside of school. Hopkins (undated) in her use of a points system found that it motivated poor attenders to attend more often.

We can thus conclude that there is evidence for a connection and possibly a causal link between planning, teaching and behaviour management on one side and attendance and classroom behaviour on the other. Since the Corrective Reading programme both carefully sequences the reading material increasing the chance of frequent success for pupils, and structures the teachers' behaviour to emit a high frequency of praise and reinforcing comments, one would speculate that one might find a greater improvement in attendance and behaviour in other lessons (English and Maths) for the experimental group as a consequence of having introduced Corrective Reading, than for the comparison group.

The experimental and comparison groups were rendered comparable in pre-test measures of the reading, behaviour and attendance by the use of the analysis of covariance.

4. <u>Social disadvantage</u>. 36 per cent of the experimental group and 38 per cent of the comparison group were from socially disadvantaged homes, as indicated by receipt of free school meals. This was an attempt to equate support from home for the two groups.

5. <u>Teacher's education</u>. Both groups were taught by the second author but the comparison group was taught two lessons per week by a second teacher. The groups were thus obviously dissimilar in this respect. Both teachers had similar lengths of teaching experience in secondary schools but the teacher of the comparison group, though not being new to this school, had no experience of teaching remedial children, whereas that of the experimental teacher was extensive.

6. <u>Teacher's experience</u>. The experimental group teacher was trained in the use of Corrective Reading as described earlier. The comparison group teacher, not having used the remedial equipment before, was not taught how to use it but just given advice on the procedure used in its operation.

7. <u>Support</u>. The experimental teacher was extensively involved in the planning and implementation of this project and consequently had much contact with the first

author, headmaster and to a lesser extent the remedial adviser concerning the project. The comparison group teacher did not have any such contact with the psychologist.

Contact between the experimental teacher (in fact the second author) and the psychologist (the first author) can be divided into that occurring before the Corrective Reading programme was started and that occurring during its operation. Before the programme started 13 meetings occurred between May and October 1979. This was a period of 16 working weeks; consequently meetings were nearly at the rate of one per week. During the programme seven meetings occurred between January and October 1980. Therefore there were seven meetings in 8 months; approximately at a rate of one per month. The total was 20 meetings in all. Further meetings are planned to arrange the second phase of the project.

The reason for so much concern over the extent of support from an outside agency in the implementation of this programme is that Maggs and Morath (1975) demonstrate differences in gains in language level of children taught using DISTAR Language 1 between schools. One school showed good gains whilst three others showed poor gains. Maggs and Morath suggest that the difference occurred because of differences in the extent of monitoring and support for the DISTAR teachers from within the schools and a researcher from outside. It can be concluded that DISTAR programmes, and one might include the Corrective Reading programmes also, can fail to show results when not taught as prescribed and when the teacher is not supported intensively.

The following process variables were considered:
1. <u>Time spent on the programme</u>. The experimental group was given 57 lessons in 5 months. They reached lesson 26 of Corrective Reading, indicating that it was taking approximately two lessons to cover one Corrective Reading lesson. Both groups received the same number of lessons.

Four lessons a week were taught but on only 3 days of the week. The experimental group received lessons on Monday, period 3, Thursday, periods 3 and 7 and Friday, period 4. The comparison group received lessons on Monday, periods 3 and 6, Thursday, period 4 and Friday, period 6. Period 6 was just before dinner-time. It was assumed that the pattern of teaching periods would not create differences between the groups. As can be seen on one day the group received two lessons. This is not exactly as SRA recommend since they suggest one lesson per day be taught. Becker (1977) indicates that more progress can be expected of students if one increases the academic engaged time.

2. Administration of the programme. Both programmes were monitored to be sure they were being used appropriately. The psychologist monitored the experimental group teacher in the use of Corrective Reading, making observational measures of student response rates, correction procedures, frequency of praise and reprimand by the teacher and the frequency with which student attention was gained before presenting a task. The inexperienced comparison group teacher was monitored by the second author to be certain that the appropriate procedures were carried out with the programme materials. Both groups received appropriately presented programmes.

3. Content and sequence of both programmes. As indicated in the introduction, Corrective Reading is a carefully task-analysed programme. The teacher has a presentation book indicating what should be written on the blackboard. The students follow the work, giving group responses with occasional individual turns. The weakest students are placed at the front in the middle. It is assumed that if these students respond correctly on individual turns then the rest probably will. Simultaneous group responding to the teacher's signal allows the teacher to identify quickly students who have not responded or have given an incorrect response. Teaching continues until all of the group have mastered the task and only then does the teacher move on. After the blackboard work individuals read a sentence each from their student books in turn around the group. Success here was rewarded with points which in this project were cashed in for the school's house points. This worked well as a motivation system.

The school's current remedial programme as used in the present project, and in the previous year, to teach the groups described in Table 9.1, consists of:

(a) SRA reading laboratory 1c and 2a
(b) Blackwell Spelling Workshop
(c) Wolverhampton Supply Company phonic programme
(d) Blackwell Talk, Write and Spell
(e) Handwriting practice
(f) General language work (spoken and written).

Much of this material was used for individualised instruction by both comparison group teachers which is very different from the group instruction of Corrective Reading. No points system was used. Continuity between the work of both teachers to the comparison group was maintained to a degree. Much of the remedial materials used were kits of a sequential nature allowing a student to carry on with the second teacher where he left off with the first. The handwriting practice and general language work had less continuity, as detailed discussions between the teachers on what had been taught and what should come next were not held.

The following outcome variables were considered:

(1) The post-test reading ages
(2) Final attendance rating
(3) Final behaviour rating

These will be described in the discussion.

Experimental group variables:

Subjects:	Four boys, seven girls (N = 11) from class 1 to 3.
Socially disadvantaged:	(receiving free school meals) 36 per cent of the group.
Teacher:	Experienced in remedial work, trained to use Corrective Reading.
Materials:	Corrective Reading teacher and student books for group teaching.
Support from Psychologist:	20 meetings over 17 months.
Time spent on the programme:	Four periods per week for 5 months.
Testing:	The Daniels and Diack test of reading experience (a group test) was administered by the second author. The Corrective Reading placement test was administered by the first author.

Comparison group variables:

Subjects:	Six boys, two girls (N = 8) from class 1 to 4.

Socially
disadvantaged: (receiving free school meals) 38 per cent of the group.

Teachers: Two periods from the experimental group teacher and two periods with a second teacher (not experienced in remedial work and not specifically trained but only given advice in the use of the school's current remedial materials).

Materials: Largely commercially available kits of individualised work.

Support from
Psychologist: Nil

Time spent on
the programme: Four periods per week for 5 months

Testing: As for experimental group.

In summary then, the two groups were comparable except for the sex distribution, the comparison group having two teachers and one of these being inexperienced in remedial work, and support from the psychologist. The difference in the training the teachers received is not a source of difference since monitoring indicated that both groups received adequately implemented programmes.

Installation

The objective was to match the characteristics of the innovation with those of the adopting institution. Corrective Reading demands 30 to 40 minutes teaching to a group of up to 15 pupils every day, and a school must adjust its timetable to accommodate as much as possible. The method of achieving this objective was through the initial verbal contract with the school, that they would take up Corrective Reading if it showed good results, and also through the use of this project. An extra member of staff was used to facilitate timetable adjustments to accommodate Corrective Reading.

Institutionalisation

The innovation must be assimilated and become an integral and accepted component of the receiving institution. The innovation becomes current practice maintained, independent from the agency who initiated the innovation. This probably is one of the most difficult steps to achieve. Many a project can be maintained in a school with ample input from outside, but will it continue when this input is faded out? Will it continue once the key teacher has left? The innovation must have a self-sustaining maintenance system in which staff losses are replaced by newly trained staff. For the present project this step has not yet been achieved, but hopeful signs are the enthusiasm of the headteacher and remedial teacher for Corrective Reading and the pre-testing, placement testing and staff replacement training undertaken in recent months independent of the school psychological service.

The method used here was a phased withdrawal by the senior author from the tasks required of the project ensuring that the remedial teacher had learnt or been taught how to carry them out independently. The final step will be the writing up of the second phase of the experiment having collected follow-up reading scores.

Methods and arrangements (Stage 3)

As has been seen, different methods or sets of arrangements can exist for each objective. For the general approach to the method of achieving the sequence of objectives, factors that may influence the likelihood of a psychologist undertaking innovative work (Gregory, 1981b) and the guidelines for intervening in organisations proposed by Georgiades and Phillimore (1975) and expanded by Gregory (1980c) were taken into careful consideration in this planning stage. Luthans and Kreitner (1975) indicate how organisational behaviour is influenced by its consequences and hence the teacher implementing Corrective Reading was encouraged to take on small steps at a time with contingent reinforcements from the senior author and with the knowledge that a successfully completed project would lead to a jointly written paper presented to the local education authority. Visits from interested teachers and students also served to reinforce the project teacher.

The senior author was well known to the headteacher and a number of school staff. The project was proposed following discussion of the direct instruction Follow-through results and Corrective Reading results quoted by Thorne

(1978), between the two authors and the headteacher.

Methods and internal evaluation (Stages 4 and 5)

Stages 4 and 5 of Figure 9.1 will be examined together at this point and the following questions asked:

Stage 4. To what extent were the methods and arrangements used to achieve the objectives satisfactory? This cannot be fully answered without reference to Stage 5.

Stage 5. Were the objectives set in Stage 2 achieved?

Of the six objectives, five definitely were achieved. Dissemination was assumed to have been achieved because of the teacher's continued interest in Corrective Reading. Since the objective was achieved the method used, namely discussing the Corrective Reading sampler and research papers with the remedial teacher and SRA representative, was considered satisfactory.

The demonstration objective was achieved, and consequently the method (a demonstration lesson from an SRA trainer) was assumed satisfactory. It was realised that other methods could have been used instead, i.e., a video of a Corrective Reading lesson, or a demonstration at another secondary school.

The training objective might have been assessed before the teaching of Corrective Reading commenced. This was not possible, so an observation of one of the first lessons was undertaken involving the following dimensions; signalling, frequency of response from pupils, seating of pupils and rate of verbal reinforcement. These were all found to be satisfactory. Since the training objective was achieved the method, of having the teacher practise with another member of staff and then with good pupils, was considered satisfactory.

The trial objective, to evaluate the effectiveness of Corrective Reading, has been achieved (see Tables 9.2 and 9.3). They show the gains in reading scores for the experimental and comparison groups. Whilst the comparison group, on average, gained 0.23 of a year, the experimental group, on average, gained nine times more, namely 1.8 years in a period of 5 months (or less than 12 weeks assuming five lessons per week and 57 lessons in all). The pupils were less than a quarter of the way through the programme. It is not clear why the comparison group shows smaller gains than last year's group in Table 9.1. It may be due to the

Table 9.2: Experimental group pre- and post-test reading ages, school attendance and behaviour questionnaire scores

Subjects	Age Jan. 1980	Sex	Corrective reading placement test		Reading Ages REA	
			Errors	Placement	Jan. 1980 pre-test	June 1980 post-test
1	12-3	M	15.0	B1	7.7	9.1
2	11-8	F	8.0	B1	8.4	11.2
3	11-4	M	15.0	B1	8.3	10.3
4	12-0	F	35.0	B1	8.6	9.5
5	11-7	F	21.0	B1	7.9	10.0
6	11-10	M	33.0	B1	8.4	10.0
7	11-11	M	11.0	B61	8.4	11.2
8	11-5	F	17.0	B1	8.6	10.0
9	11-9	F	4.0	C1	8.1	9.3
10	11-10	F	10.0	B1	8.6	9.7
11	11-5	F	–	C1	8.7	10.3
Mean	11-9		16.9		8.3	10.1
Mean Boys (4)	11-10		18.5		8.2	10.15
Mean Girls (7)	11-6		15.8		8.4	10.00

Table 9.2: continued

Subjects	Gain in years	Number of lessons completed	School attendance		Rutter Behaviour Questionnaire score	
			Term 1 (146) pre-test Y	Term 2 + 3 (162) post-test X	Pre-test Y	Post-test X
1	1.4	57	141	160	1.0	1.0
2	2.8	55	141	158	0.5	1.0
3	2.0	55	126	156	0.5	3.0
4	0.9	57	139	162	2.0	1.5
5	2.1	55	134	159	0.5	0.5
6	1.6	53	114	152	1.0	3.0
7	2.8	53	136	156	1.0	0.0
8	1.4	57	128	160	0.5	0.0
9	1.2	44	122	130	1.0	0.0
10	1.1	55	131	158	0.0	0.0
11	1.6	56	132	160	0.0	0.0
Mean	1.8***		131.27	155.5*	0.73	0.91**
Mean Boys (4)	1.95					
Mean Girls (7)	1.60					

* $P < 0.05$ F = 6.934 for degrees of freedom of 1 and 16 comparing attendance scores (post-test X) of the experimental group with the comparison group, having adjusted for uncontrolled Y (pre-test score).

** $P < 0.01$ F = 9.04 for degrees of freedom 1 and 16 comparing Rutter Questionnaire scores (post-test X) of the experimental group with the comparison group, having adjusted for uncontrolled Y (Rutter Questionnaire pre-test score).

*** $P < 0.001$ F = 20.589 for degrees of freedom 1 and 16 comparing the reading gains of the experimental group with those of the comparison group.

Note: REA = Daniels and Diack test of grading reading experience

Table 9.3: Comparison group pre- and post-test reading ages, school attendance and behaviour questionnaire scores

| Subjects | Age Jan. 1980 | Sex | Corrective reading placement test | | Reading ages REA | |
			Errors	Placement	Jan. 1980 pre-test	June 1980 post-test
1	12–3	M	19.0	B1	7.8	7.1
2	11–7	F	24.0	B1	7.4	7.6
3	11–8	M	13.0	B1	8.8	9.0
4	11–11	M	10.0	B61	8.3	8.2
5	12–3	F	11.0	B1	7.0	7.6
6	11–11	M	20.0	B1	7.1	7.4
7	11–5	M	17.0	B1	7.6	7.8
8	11–9	M	5.0	C1	8.8	10.0
Mean	11–10		14.9		7.85	8.08
Mean boys (6)	11–10		14.0		8.07	8.25
Mean girls (2)	11–11		17.5		7.20	7.60

Table 9.3: continued

Subjects	Gain in years	School attendance		Rutter Behaviour Questionnaire score	
		Term 1 (146) pre-test Y	Term 2 + 3 (162) post-test X	Pre-test Y	Post-test X
1	-0.7	133	150	3.0	9.0
2	0.2	146	162	2.0	1.5
3	0.2	136	152	0.0	2.5
4	-0.1	144	148	0.5	2.5
5	0.6	116	123	1.5	2.0
6	0.3	80	128	0.5	4.0
7	0.2	138	147	1.5	5.5
8	1.2	145	152	0.0	3.0
Mean	0.23***	129.75	145.25*	1.125	3.75**
Mean boys (6)	0.18				
Mean girls (2)	0.40				

* $P < 0.05$ F = 6.934 for degrees of 1 and 16 comparing attendance scores (post-test X) of the experimental group with the comparison group, having adjusted for uncontrolled Y (pre-test attendance score).

** $P < 0.01$ F = 9.04 for degrees of freedom 1 and 16 comparing Rutter Questionnaire scores (post-test X) of the experimental group with the comparison group, having adjusted for uncontrolled Y (Rutter Questionnaire pre-test score).

*** $P < 0.001$ F = 20.589 for degrees of freedom 1 and 16 comparing the reading gains of the experimental group with those of the comparison group.

Note: REA = Daniels and Diack test of graded reading experience comparison group having had two teachers.

However, some individuals in the experimental group were making nearly 3 years' progress. The boys made an average gain of 1.95 years whilst the girls on average made 1.60 years. It is not immediately clear why the girls should not do quite as well as the boys since the girls started with a better average error rate on the placement test and a slightly higher pre-test reading age.

Since the trial objective was achieved, the method used to achieve it, i.e., the particular evaluation design (described by Fitzgibbon and Lyons-Morris (1978) as a non-equivalent control group pre-test and post-design) with the analysis of covariance, is taken to have been appropriate.

There was concern over the use of this particular statistic because the two groups were not constituted by random assignment, but it was felt safe to assume that the members of the two groups were so similar as to be little different from randomly assigned groups anyway (Fitz-Gibbon and Lyons-Morris, 1978, p. 91).

For the first question (asked in the trial objective), 'In what ways and to what extent is the Corrective Reading programme better than what was done before?', it was apparent that the Corrective Reading programme supported a positive behaviour management style in the teacher, more so than the current reading programme used. This management system, involving contracting and a points system, fitted well with the school's house point system. The continuity of work was greater with the Corrective Reading programme than would be possible using a number of different kits and materials.

The second question, asking 'What additional, possibly unanticipated effects had the Corrective Reading programme had and to what extent were they better or worse than the previous way things were done?', can be answered in that the programme increased the dialogue between the Remedial and English departments in the school. The English department attended the SRA demonstration of Corrective Reading. Timetabling one teacher to a group of about 12 students to meet five times a week was problematic. Staff at a large comprehensive school in Tyneside overcame this problem by banding. Two classes (of 20-25) made up the 'C' band of below average students. The English periods for these two classes were timetabled for three teachers not two for the first, second and third-year groups. This allowed a Corrective Reading group for each year.

Also staff time required for hearing students read following a Corrective Reading lesson was difficult to find and consequently it was done in the next lesson, resulting in one Corrective Reading lesson being completed in two periods. Hopkins (undated) overcomes this problem of checking by awarding the checkers' jobs to the best performing students each lesson. This saved some time.

Unanticipated to a degree at the outset, was the cost of the consumable Corrective Reading student materials. The remedial department had to budget for these in the forthcoming academic year.

Although not specifically assessed, pupils using the Corrective Reading programme did express an enthusiasm for reading not seen with the comparison group.

Apparent from Tables 9.2 and 9.3 are the findings that school attendance for the experimental group improved significantly more than for the comparison group. This is particularly significant because in a previous year children withdrawn from mixed ability classes for extra tuition and taught (by whichever teacher was free at the time) on work set by the remedial teacher were found to attend school much less often than their classmates, and to show deteriorating attendance through the year (Gregory, 1981c).

Taking the comparison group alone pre- and post-attendances remained the same,

i.e. 88 per cent (129.75/146) and 89 per cent (145.25/162).

This suggests that the problem of the declining attendance of pupils withdrawn from mixed ability clases, described in Gregory (1983), can be overcome by making the withdrawal from streamed classes to work with particular teachers, on structured remedial work that has continuity.

Tables 9.2 and 9.3 show that there is a significant difference in the change of behaviour (as rated on the Rutter Children's Behaviour Questionnaire by the English and Maths teachers) for the two groups. That of the experimental group worsened very slightly - whilst that of the comparison group did so markedly.

The installation objective was achieved when Corrective Reading lessons were timetabled for the second year of the project. The method used was a verbal contract that Corrective Reading would be used if the results were good enough. A draft copy of this report was also part of the method and helped decide the remedial adviser to fund materials required to run the project for a second year.

For the institutionalisation objective, the method cannot yet be evaluated since this objective has not yet been achieved.

External evaluation (Stage 6)

It is at this point that one refers back to the stated needs in Stage 1, to see whether these have been fulfilled. This can be done in part by reference to the trial results. These indicate gains nine times greater in the experimental group compared with the comparison group and also maintained good behaviour and improved attendances. These, once Corrective Reading is institutionalised, will fulfil some of the stated needs.

DISCUSSION

The first and second purposes of providing evaluative data concerning the effectiveness of Corrective Reading and that of bringing about organisational change in school, have been fulfilled to a degree. The headteacher made arrangements for the programme to run for a second year. Again pre- and post-test reading scores will be collected in order to monitor the success of this second phase. Evaluation is to be an integral part of this phase and largely to be carried out by the second author. This goes some way towards fulfilling the third purpose of this action-research, namely assisting a school in carrying out its own evaluation.

Fourthly, the purpose of demonstrating an alternative model of working for an educational psychologist has been exemplified. Had the remedial problems of the school been dealt with as individual referrals, probably at least as much time could have been spent on the problems as was incurred via this project approach and, more importantly, the problem would have been conceived at an individual rather than at the organisational level. Had this happened it would have been unlikely that organisational solutions, such as the use of Corrective Reading for a trial period, an extra teacher and finance, would have been put forward.

Hawthorne effects inflate experimental results as a

consequence of the extra attention being paid to the experimental group. This effect probably was at work in this project with respect to the reading, and judgment as to its extent will only be gauged after Corrective Reading has run another year, allowing for initial enthusiasm to die down. However, the evaluator may be less concerned with such effects than the researcher (Stufflebeam et al. 1971) since the evaluator may only want to demonstrate gains in reading skill, being less concerned with the minutiae of finding out which aspects of the programme caused it.

The Corrective Reading programme gained much better results with the remedial pupils in this school's conditions than did the school's alternative. The comparison and experimental groups were comparable except for sex distribution, the comparison group having two teachers and one of these being inexperienced in remedial work, and psychologist support both before and during the experiment. It may be that for Corrective Reading to gain these results such support is paramount. In subsequent experiments it would be interesting to reduce this support and see how this affects teaching skills and reading gains. DISTAR programmes gained their impressive results in the Follow-through programme with an extensive teacher-training and support system and high academic engaged time, i.e., one lesson per day being taught (Becker, 1977). It may be that there is a point beyond which one cannot go in reducing training, support and academic engaged time before reading gains suffer drastically.

Thus with this comparison group, and assuming minimal differences between the groups arising from the variables for which the groups were not comparable, one is now able to say tentatively and with some reservation that Corrective Reading gains these results at a time and under similar conditions under which the school's current remedial programme has gains which are nine times less.

The results of this present study suggest it would be well worth testing and following up Corrective Reading in this and other remedial departments of comprehensive schools.

CONCLUSION

The results of this paper accord well with those of Rutter et al. (1979). Use of the Corrective Reading programme had the side-effect of maintaining the good behaviour and improving the attendance of the experimental group. The Corrective Reading programme provides a well-designed reading course and an effective behaviour management system. These two underpin the interaction between student and teacher. If the aim is to improve behaviour and attendance then one might start with improving the student-teacher interaction or relationship.

REFERENCES

Ainscow, M., Gardner, J., Bond, J. and Tweddle, D. (1978) 'The development of a three-part evaluation procedure for inset courses.' British Journal In-Service Education, 4, 184-90

Arends, R.I. and Arends, J.H. (1977) Systems Change Strategies in Educational Settings. London: Human Science Press

Becker, W.C. (1977) 'Teaching reading and language to the disadvantaged - what we have learned from field research.' Harvard Educational Review, 47, 518-43

Becker, W.C., Engelmann, S., Carnine, D.W. and Maggs, A. (1981) 'Direct instruction technology - making learning happen.' Karolz, P. and Steffen, J.J. (eds), Advances in Child Behaviour and Therapy, Volume 2. New York: Gardner Press

Daniels, J.C. and Diack, H. (1972) The Standard Reading Tests. London: Chatto and Windus

Fitz-Gibbon, C.T. and Lyons-Morris, L. (1978) How to Design a Program Evaluation. London: Sage

Gagne, R.M. and Briggs, L.J. (1974) Principles of Instructional Design. London: Holt, Rinehart and Winston

Georgiades, N.J. and Phillimore, L. (1975) 'The myth of the hero-innovator and alternative strategies for organisational change.' Kiernan, C. and Woodford F.P. (eds), Behaviour Modification with the Severely Retarded. Amsterdam: Scientific Publishers

Glen, F. (1975) The Social Psychology of Organisations. London: Methuen

Gordon, M.B. (1971) Distar Instructional System: Summaries of case studies on effectiveness of Distar Instructional System. Henley-on-Thames: Science Research Associates

Gregory, R.P. (1980a) 'Truancy. A plan for school-based action-research.' The Journal of the Association of Educational Psychologists 5(3), 30-4

Gregory, R.P. (1980b) 'Disadvantaged parents and contact with secondary school.' Therapeutic Education, 8(2), 23-6

Gregory, R.P. (1980c) 'Planning intervention in a secondary school.' Paper read at the BPS Division of Educational and Child Psychology Course, January 1980, Southampton University

Gregory, R.P. (1981a) 'Planning and evaluating a parents' evening in a secondary school.' Comprehensive Education, 42, 24-5

Gregory, R.P. (1981b) 'Educational psychologists and innovation.' McPherson, I. and Sutton, A. (eds), Reconstructing Psychological Practice. London: Croom Helm

Gregory, R.P. (1982) 'Attendance, social disadvantage and school organisation. A comparison of the first-year intake of two comprehensive schools.' Journal of the Association of Educational Psychologists, 5, 10, 56-60

Gregory, R.P. (1983) 'Examining a secondary school's withdrawal system of help for pupils with remedial problems. An example of within-school evaluation.' Journal of Applied Educational Studies, 12, 1, 44-55

Gregory, R.P., Meredith, P. and Woodward, A. (1982) 'Parental involvement in secondary school.' Journal of the Association of Educational Psychologists, 5, 8, 54-60

Hopkins, L. (undated) Corrective Reading: A Teacher's Viewpoint. Henley-on-Thames: Science Research Associates

Katz, D. and Kahn, R.L. (1978) The Social Psychology of Organisation. New York: Wiley

Luthans, F. and Kreitner, R. (1975) Organisational Behaviour Modification. Brighton: Scott, Foresman and Co.

Maggs, A. and Maggs, R. (1979) 'Direct instructional research in Australia.' American Journal of Special Educational Technology, 11, 3, 26-4

Maggs, A., Moore, J., Hawke, H. and Cunliffe, L. (undated) 'Aboriginal education: preparing children for self determination - a common goal for all children.' Unpublished paper. School of Education, Macquarie University, NSW

Maggs, A. and Morath, P. (1975) Use of Experimental Kits

among Children with Moderate Mental Retardation.
Schools Commission File No. 74/33. Special Education
Centre, Macquarie University, NSW

Maggs, A. and Murdoch, R. (1979) 'Teaching low performers
in upper primary and lower secondary to read by direct
instruction methods.' Reading Education, 1, 35-9

Margulies, N. and Wallace, J. (1973) Organisational Change.
Techniques and Applications. Brighton: Scott, Foresman
and Co.

McNemar, Q. (1962) Psychological Statistics. London: Wiley

Mehrens, W.A. and Lehmann, I.J. (1973) Measurement and
Evaluation in Education and Psychology. New York:
Holt, Rinehart and Winston

Morrish, I. (1976) Aspects of Educational Change. London:
George Allen and Unwin

Munro, R.G. (1977) Innovation: Success or Failure. London:
Hodder and Stoughton

Parlett, M. and Hamilton, D. (1978) 'Evaluation as
illumination.' Hartley, J. and Davies, I. (eds),
Contribution to an Educational Technology. London:
Kogan Page

Rutter, R.M. (1967) 'A children's behaviour questionnaire for
completion by teachers: preliminary findings.' Journal
of Child Psychology and Psychiatry. 8, 1-11

Rutter, R.M., Maughan, B., Mortimore, P. and Ouston, J.
(1979) Fifteen Thousand Hours. Secondary Schools and
their Effects on Children. London: Open Books

Stufflebeam, D.I., Foley, W.J., Gephart, W.J., Guba, E.G.,
Hammond, R.I., Merriman, O.H. and Provus, M.M.
(1971) Educational Evaluation and Decision Making.
Itasca, Ill: Peacock

Sutton, A. (1977) 'Special education and social disadvantage.'
Paper presented at seminar on special education and
social disadvantage, 22 June, at Centre for Child Study,
University of Birmingham

Thorne, M.T. (1978) 'Payment for reading. The use of the
Corrective Reading scheme with junior maladjusted
boys.' Remedial Education, 13(2), 87-90

Tizard, J. (1976) 'Psychology and social policy.' Bulletin of
British Psychological Society, 29, 225-34

Topping, K. (1977) 'Investigations of aspects of the role and
functioning of a city psychological service.' Unpublished
dissertation, Department of Psychology. University of
Nottingham

APPENDICES

Appendix 1: Analysis of variance for X variable (post-test reading score) by covariance adjusted for uncontrolled Y variable (pre-test reading score)

		Total	Within	Between
1	Sum of product	9.21	4.78320	4.4268
2	Sum of squares: X	29.0968	11.17575	17.9211
3	Sum of squares: Y	5.6611	4.565	1.0961
4	df	N-1	N-G	G-1
		18	17	1
5	Correlation	0.7183	0.6700	0.9995
5a	df for r	N-2	N-G-1	G-2
		17	16	0
6	Adjusted (X^2)	14.1120	6.1708	7.9412
7	df	17	16	1

F = 20.589 for df 1 and 16 is significant at beyond the 0.001 level

Appendix 2: Analysis of variance for X variable (post-test attendance score term 2 plus 3) by covariance adjusted for uncontrolled Y variable (pre-test attendance score term 1)

		Total	Within	Between
1	Sum of products	2135.474	2062.56	72.61
2	Sum of squares: X	2479.16	1988.23	490.93
3	Sum of squares: Y	4194.42	4183.68	10.74
4	df	N-1	N-G	G-1
		18	17	1
5	Correlation	0.6622	0.7152	0.9996
5a	df for r	N-2	N-G-1	G-2
		17	16	0
6	Adjusted (X^2)	1391.9419	971.0893	420.8526
7	df	17	16	1

F = 6.934 for df. 1 and 16 is significant between 0.05 and 0.01 levels

Appendix 3: Analysis of variance for X variable (post-test Rutter Questionnaire score) by covariance adjusted for uncontrolled Y variable (pre-test Rutter Questionnaire score)

		Total	Within	Between
1	Sum of products	12.46	7.23	5.23
2	Sum of squares: X	93.29	55.91	37.38
3	Sum of squares: Y	11.79	11.05	0.74
4	df	N-1	N-G	G-1
		18	17	1
5	Correlation	0.3758	0.2908	0.9943
5a	df for 4	N-2	N-G-1	G-2
		17	16	0
6	Adjusted (X^2)	80.12	51.18	28.94
7	df	17	16	1

F = 9.04 for df 1 and 16 is significant between 0.01 and 0.001 levels

Chapter Ten

THE EFFECTIVENESS OF HOME VISITS BY AN EDUCATION WELFARE OFFICER IN TREATING SCHOOL ATTENDANCE PROBLEMS*

R.P. Gregory, J. Allebon and N.M. Gregory

This article describes a project centred on a secondary school in the West Midlands. A discussion between the school's headmaster, the area education welfare officer (EWO), the school's EWO and the educational psychologist, aimed at improving the school's pupil attendance, led to the writing of a planning document linking together school-based action research on truancy (Gregory, 1980a). The assumption was that absenteeism and truancy have multiple causal factors involving the child, the home and the school. The latter is the most important from the school's point of view, in that it is only these variables that are directly under the control of the school staff. The following papers describe some research already undertaken in this school. Gregory, Hackney and Gregory (1981 and 1982) give details of improvement in classroom behaviour, attendance and reading in a group of children using the Corrective Reading Programme. Gregory, Meredith and Woodward (1982) and Gregory (1980b) describe the improvement of parents' evenings aimed at increasing pupil attendance. Further papers involving this school are Gregory (1982, 1983). The extent of research about this school should be taken as a testament to its exemplary co-operation and willingness to examine itself, rather than an indication of its problems.

The purpose of this article is threefold. Firstly it is to investigate the effectiveness of the EWO home visiting of pupils referred to the EWO by the school for attendance

*Reprinted from Research in Education, 32, 51-65, 1984. Published by kind permission of Research in Education published by Manchester University Press

problems. Secondly, it documents the relatively rare occurrence of the local authority (LEA) education welfare department and LEA psychological service getting together on a joint project to undertake school-based evaluation of current practice, something which ideally should be routine in all schools. Thirdly, it exemplifies a role which is more the scientist or action researcher than is often the case with the traditional role of the educational psychologist, who can be largely involved in casework.

An extensive search of the literature has revealed that the role of the EWO falls into a number of categories. A surprise is the contrast between the extensive number of references on absenteeism and truancy and their relative paucity on the role of the EWO. In turn within the latter one finds much about the expectations authors have of the role but much less describing the actual day to day work of an EWO, there being a difference between what people are said to do and what they actually do. Firstly, however, the Ralphs report (1974), Pedley (1975), Clarke (1976), Davis (1976), McMillan (1977), Watkins and Derrick (1977), Stoll (1979) and Milner (1980) describe the history of EWOs, their current varied role and their training needs.

Secondly, Sutton (1971, 1975, 1978), Galloway (1976) and Gregory (1980a) appear to be the only contributions by educational psychologists discussing the need for psychological services to be involved in activities like surveys of prevalence, evaluation of intervention and investigation of school factors in attendance problems, etc., which would bring direct liaison with the LEA education welfare department.

Thirdly, Hart (1977) and Woodward and Allebon (1977) argue for better links between EWOs and school staff, whilst Myers (n.d.) voices the need for EWOs to reduce their case load in order to create time to work more intensively on the more complex problems.

Fourthly, regarding intervention and treatment, Pritchard (1974) looks at the characteristics of an EWO's hard-core case load, concluding that, in order to deliver improved intervention and treatment, EWOs need more training. Carroll (1977) is a great source of references on absenteeism. Herbert (1978) describes case studies in the treatment of school non-attenders using a behavioural approach, whilst Hersov and Berg (1980) provide an extensive perspective on truancy and its treatment. Parker and McCoy (1977) found that a head teacher who telephoned the parents of poor-attending children, praising their attendance and deploring absence, produce sustained increases in attendance and parent-initiated contacts with the school.

Fifthly, the more specific intervention of court proceedings and their effectiveness are described by Allebon (1976), Berg et al. (1978) and Reynolds (1978), the two latter describing case adjournment as more effective in improving subsequent attendance of poor-attending children than supervision by the social services department.

Heartening is the discovery of papers (not always published) by LEA education welfare department officers trying to evaluate their own work (Allebon, 1976; Myers, n.d.; Woodward and Allebon, 1977).

METHOD

The school in which the study was based is a mixed comprehensive, previously secondary modern. It is situated in a suburb. It had four-form intake and approximately 600 pupils at the time of the data collection in 1977-78. Now it has been combined with another neighbouring secondary school. In a survey of all the first-year pupils in the year 1976-77 it was found that 60 per cent of these children were from families of five or more or one-parent families, compared to 23 per cent nationally (Wedge and Prosser, 1973). Twenty-two per cent were from disadvantaged homes as indicated by receipt of free school meals, compared to 6 per cent nationally for eleven-year-old children (Wedge and Prosser, 1973). The present sample was drawn from the first to fifth year in 1977-78 and totals 73 in all.

The senior master of the school, on Friday afternoons, examined all the registers and by viewing the attendance figures selected the absence slips of those who had been off school. No particular attempt was made to select the truants or the worst non-attenders, as will be confirmed later. Some 120 absence slips were passed to the EWO on Monday morning. From these he usually selected 80 to visit. At no point was the school counsellor consulted. She knew many of the children in the school who had family, social, attendance or behaviour problems.

For the experiment, in a particular week these 80 referrals to the EWO were randomly assigned to two groups - an experimental group who were to be visited as often as was usually necessary by the school EWO, and a control group who were not to be visited at all. This assignment was done blind by the area EWO and the school psychologist - the third and first authors respectively. Neither knew of the children's family or attendance history. A grid was made out with two cells per class, four classes per year and five years, first to fifth year, for the experimental and control groups, making 80 cells in all, 40 per group. The absence slips were thoroughly shuffled and the first appropriate child assigned first to the first-year experimental group, then the control group, so filling the cells from first year to fifth with alternate assignment. Not all cells were filled, resulting in the experimental group having 37 cases (19 boys, 18 girls) whilst the control group had 36 cases (22 boys, 14 girls).

It was assumed that this method of assignment was random and resulted in two equivalent groups. This is later confirmed. The assignment here involved stratifying the cases by class and year. One might also include 'sex' if the experiment were to be repeated. In the present case, when selecting from 80, there were not enough referrals to fill all the cells with equal numbers of boys and girls.

The experimental design adopted is a pre- and post-test equivalent group design, using two pre-test measures (Cook and Campbell, 1979). The attendance for September to December 1977 and 5-24 January 1978 constitute the two pre-test measures.

The referrals were collected by the senior master on Friday afternoon, 24 February 1978, and passed to the EWO on Monday 27 February. In every case the senior master passed the pupil referrals to the EWO because there was concern that there was an attendance problem or possible truancy.

All pupils in the experimental group were visited in the first week, 28 February to 3 March, in order to compare the pupils' speed of return to school (after absence and the first visits), starting Monday 6 March. Hence the post-test measure of attendance runs from Monday 6 March to the end of term, Wednesday 22 March. Attendance in the week ending 3 March was omitted in order to count the post-test attendance from a common date for both groups. Post-test attendance stopped at the holidays, as running into a second term after a long holiday would have introduced further unwanted variables. Holidays may affect attendance levels in the first weeks after a holiday. It was felt that nearly two and a half weeks should show some difference in attendance between the two groups.

The sources of data were school attendance registers, medical cards, absence slips and school records. There were two hypotheses: (1) that the experimental group would show a quicker return to school following absence and the EWO home visiting than the control group; (2) that the experimental group would show improved attendance for the post-test period as compared to the control group as a consequence of being visited. It was judged that both absence due to illness and truancy would be shorter for the experimental group than the control group.

The half-days for term one, September to December 1977, and those from 6 January to 24 February 1978 were added together to give a single pre-test measure of attendance. The two groups were rendered comparable statistically on the pre-test data whilst compared on their post-test measure using the analysis of covariance (ANCOVA) (McNemar, 1962).

In order to allow visual comparison Figure 10.1 shows the relationship between the two groups in terms of mean percentage attendance. However, in the statistical analysis half-days were used, not percentage attendance, since the latter artificially reduces the variance.

The EWO who carried out the visits could probably be said to represent the traditional style of EWOs. He had been in the service 16 years at the time of data collection and on entry had received no particular training but had attended some subsequent in-service training courses.

RESULTS

Comparability of experimental and control groups

In any experiment with equivalent groups every effort must be made to show that the groups are comparable, to avoid the accusation that any treatment effect might result from differences between the groups at pre-test. From Figure 10.1 both the pre-test measures are within a few per cent of each other and vary together. Hence one can conclude the groups are comparable on this variable. Any doubt is taken care of by the use of the ANCOVA statistic. Table 10.1 shows that on other variables, such as the pupil coming from a one-parent family, large (five or more) or disadvantaged

Table 10.1: A comparison of sex distribution and social variables for the experimental and control groups

	Boys	Girls	One-parent family	Five or more children in family	Three or four children in family	Free school meals
				Percentage number of pupils having		
Experimental group (N = 37)	18	19	14	32 (43)	30	14
Control group (N = 36)	22	14	22	25 (44)	33	11

Figure 10.1: Mean percentage attendances for control and experimental groups and sub-groups

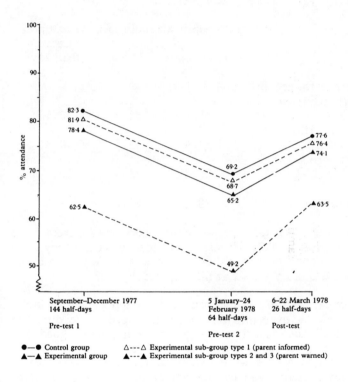

family (as indicated by receipt of free school meals), the two groups are broadly comparable. In fact for the experimental and control groups 43 and 44 per cent respectively were from one-parent or large families (Table 10.2).

Attrition in the experimental group, where four subjects were lost because although their houses were visited no contact with either parent was made, was not a great problem. It has not greatly altered the composition of

Table 10.2: A comparison of the percentage number of pupils showing a good (91 per cent or more) attendance, average (75-90 per cent) attendance and poor (less than 75 per cent) attendance for the total sample. Period: pre-test, i.e. term 1, September-December 1977

| | % pupils attending for (% of time) | | |
	91 or more	75-90	Less than 75
Experimental group:			
Before attrition (N = 37)	35.2	32.4	32.4
After attrition (N = 33)	36.4	33.3	30.3
Control group (N = 36)	22.2	58.3	19.5
Total sample (N = 73)	28.8	45.2	26.0

Note: For pre-test 1 attrition occurred from the experimental group (four subjects) because though they were visited no contact with either parent was made by the EWO, or the EWO did not visit at all (one case)

the experimental group on the attendance variable. However, the experimental and control groups do differ in respect of the experimental group having more good and more poor attenders than the control group.

The two groups were examined for any differences in previous action taken by the school before the referral of the pupil to the EWO. Table 10.3 shows that there are some differences between the two groups, the control group having a larger proportion where no previous action was taken. However, overall nearly 70 per cent of referrals had had no previous action. The EWO's visit is thus for this school the first of the steps taken when concern over attendance occurs.

The pattern of visiting for the two groups for the four weeks immediately before the experimental period is indicated by Table 10.4. As can be seen, the rate is similar. Overall on average a pupil would have been receiving a visit every three to four weeks.

Table 10.3: The percentage of pupils for whom the school had taken previous action concerning attendance problems, before the current referral to the EWO

	No previous action taken	Letter to parents from school	Discussion with pupil	Parents seen in school	Change in school made for the pupil	Combination of the others	Total
Experimental group (N = 21)	52.4	4.8	9.5	9.5	0	23.8	100
Control group (N = 29)	79.3	0	6.9	6.9	0	6.9	100
Total sample (N = 50)	68.0	2.0	8.0	8.0	0	14.0	100

Table 10.4: The average number of visits per child per week for the experimental and control groups in the four weeks immediately before the experiment and for the experimental group during the 26 half-days of the experiment

	Average number of visits from EWO per child per week for 4 weeks before experiment		Average number of visits from EWO per child per week for the experimental period, 26 half-days	
Experimental group	(N = 31)	0.34	(N = 36)	0.74
Control group	(N = 27)	0.26	No visits	
Total	(N = 58)	0.30		

Length of absence that triggered the referral

The two groups do not differ in the length of the absence that came just before the examination of the registers by the senior master on Friday 24 February and the referral to the EWO on Monday 27th. It was this absence that primarily triggered the referral. The average period of absence was 2.9 days for the experimental group and 2.7 days for the control group. This is yet another variable for which the groups are comparable. It was found, however, when gathering this information that some children were off school for a day or two, returned and then were off again. The above treatment masks such behaviour.

Thus it can be shown that the two groups are comparable for both pre-test measures of attendance (see Figure 10.1) and frequency of one-parent or large families and also social disadvantage. (One might have expected children from such backgrounds to be more likely to have attendance problems.) For both groups the reasons for referral, the pattern of previous EWO visits and the length of absence that triggered the referral were similar. Differences between the two groups occur in their sex distribution and composition of good and poor attenders. The experimental group has a smaller proportion of pupils for whom no previous action was taken by the school. It is hoped that these differences are not great enough to render the two groups incomparable.

Quickness of EWO visit

This refers to the speed of response of the system to a child's absence. Already it has been said that the EWO visit is the school's first response to absence. The question is how many days can a child be off before he and his parents are visited? Such data can be given only for the experimental group, and since the frequency of visiting was higher than normal it may be that the quickness of response may also have been enhanced. In fact on average a child could have been off school 6.7 days before he or his family would be visited by the EWO. This lapse of time is twice the average absence period. That is why we find that 92 per cent of the children in the experimental group were back at school before the EWO had visited their home, and 94 per cent of the control group were back by the beginning of the visit's week (28 February-3 March), the week when the EWO visited all the experimental group children at least once.

EWO visits and their effects on subsequent attendance

The EWO was told to visit the experimental group no more frequently than was normal, so that the effects of normal patterns of visiting would be under investigation. More frequent visiting might be expected to have a greater effect. However, as Table 10.4 shows, the rate of visiting per child per week for the experimental period was twice as great as that prior to the experiment. Even with this increase Table 10.5 shows that no treatment effect could be found. There is no significant difference between the mean post-test measure of attendance for the visited group compared to the control group. Visiting at this frequency nearly once per week per child for two and a half weeks does not result in improved attendance.

Effects of visits on boys as compared with girls

Table 10.6 shows that the experimental and control groups for girls are similar in attendance at pre-test 1, 2 and post-test. The EWO visiting has no effect on girls' attendance. For boys, the experimental group improves from pre-test 2 to post-test by 11.8 per cent, whilst that for the control group boys improves by 6.4 per cent, i.e. only half the

141

Table 10.5

	Pre-test measure (1)	Post-test measure (2)
Experimental group (N = 33)	155.36	19.27 (3)
Control group (N = 36)	162.60	20.19 (3)

Notes:

N = 69, G = 2.

(1) Pre-test 1 and pre-test 2: mean attendance (half-days, 144 + 64, maximum 208).

(2) Mean attendance (half-days, maximum 26).

(3) $F = 0.0023$ for degrees of freedom 1 and 66; not significant. See appendix.

amount. Further experiments should look at the effects of visits on boys.

EWOs should not be over-alarmed at these findings. Fischer (1978) reviews the results of effectiveness research in five areas of professional practice: social work, psychotherapy and counselling, the penal system, psychiatric hospitalisation and education. He says:

> In all these areas the research indicates that at best professionals are operating with little or no empirical evidence validating their efforts, since lack of effectiveness was the rule rather than the exception. In addition, a pattern of deterioration was found in which clients of professionals were frequently found to do less well than people with similar problems who received no professional services whatsoever.

Characteristics of the EWO's home visits

The EWO made 69 home visits to 36 children in the experimental group in two and a half weeks. Of this 69, in only 50 cases did he make contact with the parent(s). 27.5 per cent or over a quarter were abortive in that the visit resulted in no contact with the family, even though visits were varied between the morning, afternoon and evening.

Of these 50 home visits, in 92 per cent of times contact was made with the mother. The other occasions involved mother and father or mother and child together. In 98 per

Table 10.6: Mean percentage attendances for experimental, (after attrition) control groups and boys and girls

	Pre-test 1 (1)	Pre-test 2 (2)	Post-test 3 (3)
Experimental group, boys (N = 16)	75.1	60.1	71.9
Experimental group, girls (N = 17)	81.5	69.9	76.1
Experimental group total (N = 33)	78.4	65.2	74.1
Experimental sub-groups EWO response type 1 (N = 27)	81.9	68.7	76.4
EWO response types 2 and 3 (N = 6)	62.5	49.2	63.5
Control group, boys (N = 22)	82.0	71.6	78.0
Control group, girls (N = 14)	82.6	65.4	76.9
Control group total (N = 36)	82.3	69.2	77.6

Notes:
(1) Mean percentage attendance for term, September-December 1977.
(2) Mean percentage attendance, 5 January - 24 February 1978.
(3) Mean percentage attendance, 6-22 March 1978.
EWO response type 1: informing parents of their child's absence.
EWO response type 2: warning parents about the absences.
EWO response type 3: warning parents about the possibility of being taken before local authority appeals sub-committee.

cent of visits the reason given by the parent for their child's absence was illness on the part of the child. Two per cent were for home duties. None gave truancy as a reason - and since it is unlikely that no truancy occurred at all among those 36 children - there would appear to be indirect evidence for parental collusion in truancy. Some mothers may be giving 'illness' as a reason for absence when the illness is not severe enough to warrant staying away from school, or when the child may just not want to go to school. This would be very difficult for the EWO to investigate further without involving the child's doctor.

No parent gave poverty as a reason, i.e. lack of shoes, clothing, etc. It may be that there was reticence over such an admission. No-contact visits were explained away by the parent saying that (s)he was out and the child was in bed ill and therefore did not answer the door.

The EWO's response to the parent for 74 per cent of visits was to inform (type 1 response) the parent of their child's absence. In 16 per cent of visits the parents were warned (type 2 response) and for 6 per cent they were warned of the possibility of being taken to the education authority appeals sub-committee (type 3 response). (For 4 per cent of responses the type was not recorded.) These three responses constitute three sub-categories of the treatment. To explore the possibility that 'warning' might have a different effect from being 'informed' of one's child's absence the experimental group was subdivided into two such sub-groups. Table 10.6 and Figure 10.1 show the trends. The experimental group as a whole improves from pre-test 2 to post-test by about 9 per cent; the experimental sub-group (informed) by about 8 per cent; the experimental sub-group (warnings) by 14 per cent and the control group by about 8 per cent. It is a possibility that the 'warnings' treatment is having a small effect. One might retrospectively create a matched group from the control group to test this comparison further, but it seems a limited possibility because the 'warnings' group is so small (N = 6). However, it is suggestive of a 3 x 2 experimental design with equal numbers in the 'no visits', 'informed' and 'warned' treatment groups and two levels of attender, moderate and poor, for example.

On no occasion was a parent warned about possible court proceedings, given advice about child management or welfare benefits, or given practical help re shoes or clothes, etc.

School counsellor

The school counsellor was a teacher, given relief from teaching to help children with problems in school or at home. Consequently she had extensive knowledge of children's home circumstances and could give an opinion as to whether a child was genuinely ill or truanting. Liaison between the EWO and school counsellor did not occur. If it had, then the referral load could have been reduced by omitting visits to children who were probably genuinely ill, leaving time to concentrate on supposed illegitimate absence.

The school counsellor rating of each case revealed 40.5 per cent that she felt did not warrant a visit because they were probably genuinely ill or did not lose much time from school. A similar percentage she thought did warrant a visit because their absence was probably illegitimate. However, she felt there were some 30 children who were not being visited that she knew of as being problem attenders. Certainly for some of these their absence slips were lost so that the senior master was not able to refer them to the EWO. This finding, coupled with those of Table 10.2 in which 36.4 per cent of the experimental group (and 22.2 of the control) had attendances of 91 per cent or better, suggests that it would be possible to cut the workload of the EWO drastically, leaving free time to experiment with alternative ways of working. Certainly it points to the need for the school and the EWO to plan their liaison explicitly, decide the criteria for investigating children's absence and decide the action to be taken.

Validity of results

It has been concluded that EWO home visits have had no effect on the subsequent attendance of the experimental group with this particular EWO and school. (Possibilities are that visits may have more effect on boys than girls, and that 'warnings' by the EWO may have an effect on subsequent attendance.)

A 'good' design (Cook and Campbell, 1979) has been used involving pre- and post-test measures for experimental and control groups of randomly assigned pupils, to ensure comparability. This design has, relative to other designs, few threats to internal validity (i.e. erroneously concluding that there is a causal connection between treatment and outcome - in this case, visits and subsequent attendance). To enhance this design a second pre-test measure was taken. This measure (see Figure 10.1) shows that the two groups are not growing apart at different rates. There is no selection/maturation bias (namely, the groups are not improving in attendance because pupils in the groups show a bias in the selection or are maturing at different rates). Having the first pre-test measure shows that pre-test 2 is spuriously low, probably because of seasonal variation. The second-term attendances might be affected by poor weather and winter ailments. Both the groups show similar improvements in attendances at post-test.

Statistical conclusion validity involves making conclusions about whether two variables covary or are related. One must have a relationship between two variables before one can start considering whether the one has caused the other to happen (i.e. internal validity) - for example, home visits have caused better subsequent attendance.

In this study no relationship has been found between home visits and subsequent attendance. In accepting the null hypothesis that no treatment effect exists, is one incorrectly concluding that there is no treatment effect? There are a number of threats to statistical conclusion validity, i.e. threats that can result in the wrong conclusion being drawn.

Firstly has the study been sensitive enough to permit reasonable statements about covariation of the two variables, visiting and attendance? One must question whether the sample size was great enough for detecting an effect of desired magnitude, given expected variance. One would expect a total of 69 pupils to be large enough to have shown some treatment effect if it had existed.

One must question the power of the statistic used. ANCOVA is considered to be a powerful statistic, providing a high chance that any treatment effect that exists will be detected. ANCOVA was used to correct for the difference in pre-test attendance that existed even after random assignment of the subjects. This is but one method of making allowances for the problem. However, none of these methods is completely free of criticism and controversy (Fitz-Gibbon and Lyons-Morris, 1978). The assumptions required for ANCOVA - that the dependent variable (attendance) has a distribution which does not depart too far from the normal type, and the variances of the two groups are similar - are not considered to have been broken in these data.

Figure 10.1 shows that the control group always had higher mean attendance levels than the experimental group. From visual inspection it seems unlikely that there is a treatment effect - but to be certain it was considered worth while statistically rendering the pre-test measure comparable.

As for reliability of treatment-implementation, another threat to statistical conclusion validity, the home visits were carried out, as far as the first author is aware, but no actual observational check was made.

The threat of random heterogeneity of pupils can inflate the error variance and reduce the chance of detecting a treatment effect. Pupils in any treatment group can differ on factors that are correlated with the major outcome variable, attendance in this case. Occasionally some pupils might be more affected by the treatment than others. The two groups were examined for the proportion of one-parent, large or socially disadvantaged families with the possibility in mind that home visits may be more or less effective with different types of family. Further experiments are needed to discover whether home visits are more effective with pupils from different types of families, in that heterogeneity of pupils would probably be reduced by selecting pupils with a particular family background.

The threat from the reliability of the measures can, if low, result in the erroneous conclusion that there is no treatment effect. Attendance registers were used and there is no evidence to suggest their reliability is suspect. However, a post-test measure of two and a half weeks may not have been long enough for a treatment effect to show up, though this seems doubtful. Only further experimentation with more visits over a longer period can tell us. But such experiments might run into the problems of the effects of holidays on attendance.

To avoid extraneous variables being a threat to statistical conclusion validity the study was carried out with one EWO and one school. (This, however, reduced external validity, i.e. the extent to which the results can be generalised to other EWOs and schools.) Most of the threats to statistical conclusion validity have been answered and thus it seems unlikely that in concluding there was no treatment effect one would be making an error. What is necessary is repetition of the study to see whether this conclusion applies more generally to EWOs and schools.

DISCUSSION

If nothing else, this article points up the need for this school and probably others to examine closely how they liaise with their EWO. Problems at various points in the liaison system can result in a poor attender not being picked up at an early stage. In this particular school form teachers who marked absence slips sometimes failed to return them to the register. Those children were missed when the slips and registers were examined on Friday afternoons.

When the senior master and the EWO met on a Monday morning not all the registers were always available - so other poor attenders could be missed. Already it has been found in this study that a lapse of six to seven days occurs between a child's first day off school and the EWO visiting. Failure of the system at various points can add to the delay. Considering that this school uses the EWO as first response to non-attendance, is this a quick enough response?

If the EWO was not to visit high-attending children perhaps he would have had more time to visit sooner the families of children who were low attenders. This was in fact the way this particular EWO would have preferred to work but the pressure of referrals from the school prevented this.

Because the registers list children by their 'house' or registration group rather than their teaching group, it was impossible to detect, visually, children having the same pattern of non-attendance and possibly missing school together. This was another problem.

The reason given by parents for their child's absence was almost invariably illness. EWOs thus cannot visit to check whether absence is legitimate or not, because, judging from these findings, parents do not admit to their child's truancy anyway.

REFERENCES

Allebon, J. (1976) 'The effectiveness of court proceedings for school non-attendance', unpublished paper, Birmingham Education Welfare Department

Berg, I., Consterdine, M., Hullin, R., McGuire, R. and Tyrer, S. (1978) 'The effect of two randomly allocated court procedures on truancy', British Journal of Criminology, 18, 3, 232-44

Carroll, H.C. (1977) Absenteeism in South Wales. Studies of pupils, their homes and their secondary schools. University College of Swansea: Faculty of Education

Clarke, J. (1976) 'Education welfare officers: a study of the work of the education welfare officers and consideration of future developments of the service', unpublished, University of London: Institute of Education

Cook, T.D. and Campbell, D.T. (1979) Quasi-experimentation: design and analysis issues for field settings. Chicago: Rand McNally

Davis, L. (1976) 'Education welfare: the patchwork service', Community Care, 18 February

Fischer, J. (1978) 'Does anything work?' Journal of Social Services Research, 1, 3, 215-43

Fitz-Gibbon, C.T. and Lyons-Morris, L. (1978) How to Design a Program Evaluation. London: Sage

Galloway, D. (1976) 'Size of school, socioeconomic hardship, suspension rates and persistent unjustified absence from school', British Journal of Educational Psychology, 46, 1, 40-7

Gregory, R.P. (1980a) 'Truancy: a plan for school-based action research', Journal of the Association of Educational Psychologists, 5, 3, 30-5

Gregory, R.P. (1980b) 'Disadvantaged parents and contact with secondary school', Therapeutic Education, 8, 2, 23-6

Gregory, R.P. (1982) 'Attendance, social disadvantage, remedial reading and school organisation: a comparison of two neighbouring comprehensive schools'. Journal of the Association of Educational Psychologists, 5, 10, 56-60

Gregory, R.P. (1983) 'Examining a secondary school's withdrawal system of help for pupils with remedial problems: an example of within-school evaluation', Journal of Applied Educational Studies, 12, 1, 44-55

Gregory, R.P., Hackney, C. and Gregory, N.M. (1981) 'Corrective reading programme: the use of educational technology in a secondary school'. School Psychology International, 2, 2, 21-5

Gregory, R.P., Hackney, C. and Gregory, N.M. (1982) 'Corrective reading an evaluation', British Journal of Educational Psychology, 52, 33-50

Gregory, R.P., Meredith, P.T. and Woodward, A.J. (1982) 'Parent involvement in secondary school', Journal of the Association of Educational Psychologists, 5, 8, 54-60

Hart, A. (1977) 'Hopping off', Journal of the Assistant Masters' Association, 72, 2, 38-9

Herbert, M. (1978) Conduct Disorders of Childhood and Adolescence. New York: Wiley

Hersov, L. and Berg, I. (eds) (1980) Out of School. Modern perspectives in truancy and school refusal. Chichester: Wiley

MacMillan, K. (1977) Education Welfare Strategy and Structure. London: Longman

McNemar, Q. (1962) Psychological Statistics. London: Wiley

Milner, J. (1980) 'Are EWOs a vanishing species?' Community Care, 7 August, 20-1

Myers, G. (undated) 'Education Welfare Department Research', unpublished paper, Calderdale Education Department

Parker, F.C. and McCoy, J.F. (1977) 'School-based intervention for the modification of excessive absenteeism', Psychology in the Schools, 14, 1, 84-8

Pedley, F.C. (1975) 'Beyond the truant', New Society, 20 March, 723-4

Pritchard, C. (1974) 'The EWO, truancy and school phobia', Social Work Today, 5, 5, 130-4

Ralphs report (1974) The Role and Training of Education Welfare Officers. The report of the Working Party chairman, Sir L. Ralphs. Local Government Training Board

Reynolds, D. (1978) 'Truants under suspended sentence', Community Care, 31 May, 20-2

Stoll, A.J. (1979) 'The role of the EWO, with particular reference to one local authority', unpublished dissertation, B.Phil.Ed., University of Birmingham

Sutton, A. (1971) 'A brief survey of educational psychologists' involvement with problems of school attendance, conducted in the West Midlands area', unpublished paper, Parent and Child Centre, A.H.A., Birmingham

Sutton, A. (1975) 'Children on interim care order for non-attendance at school: an essay in the use of individual case studies as a means of surveying current practice and needs', unpublished paper, Parent and Child Centre, A.H.A., Birmingham

Sutton, A. (1978) 'Theory, practice and cost in child care: implications from an individual case', Howard, Journal of Penology and Crime Prevention, 16, 3, 159-71

Watkins, R. and Derrick, D. (1977) Co-operative Care. Practice and information profiles. Centre for Information and Advice on Educational Disadvantage, 11 Anson Road, Manchester M14 5BY

Wedge, P. and Prosser, H. (1973) Born to Fail. London: National Children's Bureau, Arrow Books

Woodward, A. and Allebon, J. (1977) 'A survey of and report on absenteeism in a Birmingham secondary school', unpublished paper, Birmingham Education Welfare Department

APPENDIX

Analysis of variance for X variable (post-test attendance 6 March-22 March, 26 half-days) after the experimental group received home visits from the EWO, by covariance adjusted for uncontrolled Y variable (pre-test attendance term 1, September to December 1977, 144 half-days plus attendances from 5 January to 24 February 1978, 64 half-days, making possible total of 208 half-days).

		Total	Within	Between
1	Sum of products	7881.96	7766.06	115.90
2	Sum of squares:			
	X	2896.81	2882.18	14.63
3	Sum of squares:			
	Y	67815.91	66097.60	918.30
4	df	N-1	N-G	G-1
		68	67	1
5	Correlation	0.57	0.56	1*
5a	df for r	N-2	N-G-1	
		67	66	
6	Adjusted (X^2)	1969.79	1969.72	0.07
7	df	67	66	67-66 = 1

$$F = \frac{\text{between variance}}{\text{within variance}}$$

$$= \frac{0.0696/1}{1969.7197/66}$$

$$= \frac{0.0696}{29.844238}$$

= 0.0023 for df 1 and 66. F is not significant.

* Calculator machine error has taken the between correlation from between 0.99 and 1.00 to 1.00.

Chapter Eleven

THE PROCESS OF EDUCATIONAL INNOVATION

For me the now defunct Movement of Practising Psychologists was the spur to my becoming involved in research. The contention of this group was that if a psychologist really wanted to work in a scientific manner, which complemented casework, then there was little stopping him or her, other than having some time available, personal energy and motivation. If nothing else, this book shows that such behaviour is a possibility for a psychologist and that there is no shortage of schools or teachers willing to work in partnership with a psychologist in this way.

An interesting point to note is that such action-research cuts across a number of academic and educational topics. Knowledge of these is not absolutely essential, but it does help avoid some of the many problems which befall educational innovation.

These topics cover:

1. educational evaluation (Morris and Fitz-Gibbon, 1978)
2. experimental research design (Campbell and Stanley, 1963; Campbell, 1969; Cook and Campbell 1979; Robinson and Foster, 1979)
3. organisational psychology (Katz and Kahn, 1978)
4. systems theory (Beishon and Peters, 1976)
5. psychology of management (Margulies and Wallace, 1973; Raia, 1974; Luthans and Kreitner, 1975)
6. educational innovation (Nicholls, 1983)
7. school organisation development (Dalin and Rust, 1983)
8. school effectiveness (Reynolds, 1985)
9. school self-evaluation (Nuttall, 1986)
10. teacher self-evaluation (Baker, 1985)

11. use of internal and external change-agents to bring about change in schools (Davie, Phillips and Callely, 1985)
12. curriculum development movement (Stenhouse, 1976)
13. teacher-as-researcher movement (Bowen, Green and Pols, 1975)
14. action-research (Halsey, 1972; Nixon, 1981)

All of these distinct literatures nevertheless overlap with each other and all voice the need for schools to critically examine their practices with a view to improvement. No single elaborated theory of social change has been devised to link the multiplicity of these different elements (Morrish, 1976).

It is beyond the scope of this book to go into each of these areas and it is left to the reader to follow up particular topics of interest to him.

To understand the processes involved in this particular set of innovative studies, you will need to know the outline of my personal development, my experience and thinking.

After taking a degree in Psychology and training as a teacher at Durham University, I worked in Birmingham first in a down-town junior school teaching a bottom stream, then in a very large comprehensive mainly teaching pupils in remedial classes. I started work in a child guidance clinic in 1973 after training as an educational psychologist at Birmingham University. I was given a set of new cases to work on and allocated to visiting two social services observation and assessment (O&A) centres per week. There I saw children who were remanded in care for case-conference or court reports. Most often they were delinquents, school non-attenders, or showing behaviour problems in their families.

I was required to advise social services on the action to be taken, i.e. most often Supervision Order or Care Order. I realised I had little training for this work. I assumed I was fully trained after leaving my course, but (as one probably finds in all professions after initial training) I was not.

So I read round delinquency, school non-attendance and O&A Centre research. I found that from the cases I saw, they were most often from the most socially disadvantaged families, usually one parent. School non-attendance was usually only one of the problems.

The information on the child from his school was often poor, and frequently the attendance record was not easily available. Some schools were very supportive, others very antagonistic to the absenting pupils.

This generated my interest in school non-attendance, social disadvantage and the role of the school.

Because of my science background at university, I wanted above all to be a scientific psychologist - testing hypotheses, etc.

After three years, I moved to another clinic in Birmingham and stopped visiting O&A centres. This created a break and I resolved to work in a different way from just casework. (Worthy though casework is, it can often be a slow way of changing schools.) How though? Doing what?

CHAPTER ONE

Using a social disadvantage index in a secondary school
(Gregory, 1979)

In September 1976, the then Chief Psychologist sent me a copy of his paper Herbert (1976), concerning a social disadvantage index that could be used by a school. It involved information often easily available in schools and offered a way of selecting socially disadvantaged pupils.

My intention was to try it out on all the first-year pupils of a secondary school in order to pick out the socially disadvantaged pupils very early on. I knew that these children were at risk of failure in education, being suspended from school, going into local authority care, becoming delinquent, or having poor school attendance.

If such children could be identified early in school, staff could maybe make a special effort to get to know them and their families before problems arose in the school.

Whilst at a girls' comprehensive school working on a case, I asked the headteacher if I could go through the schools records using the index and pick out the most at-risk girls. The headteacher readily agreed. The work was done and written up between March and August 1977. (It was reinforcing to notice a citation by Pasternicki (1983), who made extensive use of the social disadvantage index described.) The names of 15 girls who were socially disadvantaged were passed to the headteacher.

It is probably not chance that this headteacher agreed to this project. I was familiar with the school and we had developed a good working relationship built up whilst working on their casework referrals. This period of socialisation whilst a head and someone in the role of external change-agent develop an understanding and trust for each other is important and it seems likely that it cannot be rushed. Often headteachers who frequently have only other heads from whom to draw support, will after this period of socialisation discuss the problems their school is having. Given that the school has the time, staff-energy and motivation to invest in an action-research project with an external change-agent, then one is close to beginning an innovation. It seems highly unlikely that a successful innovation could develop, if an external change-agent unknown to the school or headteacher just appeared with a suggested project.

It was at that time I realised how hard it was to stay with a project and see it through to the end. With this work I stopped after it was written up. I gave copies to the headteacher and discussed the positive pastoral care they could carry out.

I could have taken that project further and monitored the pastoral care given to the girls and their progress. I did not.

My work had been very interesting, but it may not have changed very much in the school.

Major conclusions of this paper were:

1. The school had a high proportion of socially disadvantaged pupils, 12%; most being in the lower bands, and making up 40% of the remedial class.
2. Social disadvantage was associated with poor pupil motivation, poor readers and poor attendance.
3. Poor readers were not associated with poor attendance.
4. The attendance of the remedial class pupils was not particularly a problem.

It may be that the organisation of upper band (two classes), lower band (two classes) and the small remedial class of ten pupils with one teacher for half the timetable, helped with the last finding.

CHAPTER TWO

<u>Examining a secondary school's withdrawal system of help for</u>
<u>pupils with remedial problems</u> (Gregory, 1983)

The next development was to repeat this exercise with a
neighbouring comprehensive - the subject of this book; to be
called the 'study school' (a third one would not agree).

Again, it was whilst in contact with the headteacher
over casework, that I described my findings in the girls'
comprehensive. The study school was mixed, drawing its
intake from the council housing estate built around it. It was
by this time July 1977.

To carry out inquiries or research into a problem in
school was part of the way the head of this school worked
and probably as a consequence it was only a small step for
him to agree to my repeating the school survey with the
social disadvantage index.

The results were written up in Gregory (1983). They
were very different from those for the first school:

1. There was much more social disadvantage amongst
   pupils - 21% in the first-year intake.
2. There was mixed-ability grouping and withdrawal for
   remedial help in the first year.

Those first-year pupils who were <u>withdrawn</u> had the <u>worst</u>
attendance.

CHAPTER THREE

<u>Attendance, social disadvantage, remedial reading and school</u>
<u>organisation. A comparison of two neighbouring compre-</u>
<u>hensive schools</u> (Gregory, 1982)

I then went on to compare the results from the two schools
in this paper. The results showed that:

i) The girls' comprehensive had better attendance than
   the study school, even when social disadvantage in both
   schools was rendered comparable statistically.
ii) Remedial girls in the first school attended better than
   the equivalent girls in the study school.

These results reinforced my feeling that some school non-attendance was probably caused directly by the way the school was organised. This was supported by Carroll (1977).

Kari et al. (1980) quoted by Steel (1985) suggest that much of the blame for the misbehaviour of pupils must be borne by the school. The work of Reynolds (1976) and Rutter et al. (1979) suggests that schools do make a difference; that some schools generate pupil problems. Steel (1985) suggests that teachers need to undertake school research in order to help them understand their situations and to control and direct change.

However, I began to realise my own lack of knowledge.

a) I was not sure of the technology of bringing about change in a school. I noticed Bob Burden's work (Burden, 1978) as a start, then later Burden (1981).
b) I realised that schools must evaluate their practices. What works in one school may not work in another. For example, mixed ability teaching may work well in some schools but not in all.
c) I needed a model to co-ordinate my thinking on factors involved in school absenteeism.

In February 1977 a new senior psychologist arrived at the centre where I worked. He was studying 'teaching by objectives' and had written a paper about planning and evaluating in-service training for teachers (Ainscow, Bond, Gardner and Tweddle, 1978).

I realised that the model might be useful for planning and evaluating anything - including action-research in a school. This gave rise to the paper, Gregory (1980a).

CHAPTER FOUR

Truancy: a plan for school-based action-research (Gregory, 1980a)

Work on this paper started in September 1977. It lists eleven major goals about absenteeism that a school might tackle. It has been my blue-print for action in this particular school.

After these first three papers were written, I saw the headteacher and head of remedial department and discussed the results very thoroughly. The remedial teacher defended his withdrawal system - being resistant to any criticism. He left us, and then the head was amazingly frank and open. I said that the poor attendance of withdrawn pupils may have something to do with the mixed ability/withdrawal system. He said they operated a different system a few years before, having A, B, C and D streams, but that had worked badly. The D stream had become a sink of behaviour problems. To solve this they changed to mixed ability grouping, instead of trying to solve the problems of streaming. The head agreed to change back to a top stream, a middle stream and two parallel remedial classes.

(With hindsight I should have evaluated this change I had helped bring about. I did not. This was a mistake.)

In the meantime in November 1977, the headteacher was producing a paper with the area education welfare officer (EWO) concerning absenteeism. I met this area education welfare officer on a number of occasions to assist my understanding of how the EWO worked in general and in particular in this school. He was, with the headteacher, setting up a 'clinic' at which teachers, the head and parents of a child who was frequently absent, met to discuss the problem. This area EWO was very concerned to see that parents invited to such a meeting in school found it a reinforcing rather than a punishing experience. This contact laid the foundations for the development of the research with the school EWO (see Chapter 10, Gregory, Allebon and Gregory, 1984). The enthusiasm of this EWO was a welcome stimulus to maintain my motivation to do that project.

Later, I met the deputy head who had just completed a MSc degree in parent-involvement in school, and was complaining of low parental attendance at parents' evenings. Because many parents collude in school non-attendance, having better parent-school contact may aid pupils' attendance. Consequently a project was developed to examine the workings of parents' evenings in the school.

Writing about curriculum innovation Macdonald and Rudduck (1971) contend that experiments go well in a school where teachers are already confronting a problem and contemplating action. This was almost the case here. The school realised they had a problem. In the experiment I simply extended the range of the schools' strategies for dealing with the problem as Macdonald and Rudduck suggest one should.

Musgrove (1971) says that the deputy head often specialises in internal communication, between the head and staff in the school. The deputy head is likely to know in detail all the different sub-groups of teachers and their thinking and values. He would therefore be valuable to consult over a proposed innovation in school.

In this instance he was indispensable. Some innovative headteachers are even deploying their deputy heads as 'change-agents' for curriculum and staff development (Stenhouse, 1976).

CHAPTER FIVE

Parents' evenings in a comprehensive school. What are they for? (Gregory, 1981)

I attended a parents' evening at the school on 18 January 1978 and talked to staff informally about their views of parents and the parents' evenings. Many staff were upset that more parents did not attend. The average attendance was about 10 per cent. Again, the coincidence of the concern of the deputy head and staff for the ways parents' evenings worked, with my interest, is noticeable.

I wrote a paper about the purpose and planning of parents' evenings and presented it to the staff at a meeting. It ran from 3.30 to 5.30 pm, partly in school time - partly after school. Pupils went home early to create time for the meeting. It was for the sole purpose of deciding the arrangements for the next parents' evening in July 1978. Many ideas came from staff. The head was amazed at their creativity. Never before had they had a problem-solving meeting like this, and the head was very pleased. Staff obviously felt the psychological safety needed for them to give their frank and unreserved opinions. Many related their experiences and the organisation of parents' evenings in other schools. The head and senior staff are to be commended for their skill in generating this atmosphere in school.

Only in retrospect do I now recognise what happened in this meeting, as what Miles (1965) calls 'organisation diagnosis and problem-solving', one of six interactive techniques appropriate for problem-solving in a school. It involves the entire staff of a school, meeting to discuss a particular problem - or even to identify problems and plan the change and implementation. Miles (1964) finds these techniques set off an attitude cycle in the participants. They are initially defensive and formal until their own psychological safety is certain. (If psychological safety does not occur and staff see that those who speak up are slapped down, rejected and punished, then the next phase, of an atmosphere of 'play', trust and reduced anxiety concerning rejection, will not occur.)

Exactly the former had happened at the study school. By the end of the meeting a new way of running and organising parents' evenings was agreed with the main aim of attracting more parents to attend.

CHAPTER SIX

Parental involvement in secondary school (Gregory, Meredith and Woodward, 1982)

The experimental parents' evening occurred in July 1978. I compiled a register of parental attendance. Because many staff thought that in the past the letter of invitation to parents for the parents' evening was not delivered by the pupils (many letters could be seen in the gutter of neighbouring streets after school), it was agreed the invitations on this occasion should be posted directly to parents by responsible fifth-year pupils. All parents were told that if they couldn't come in the evening, they could come into school during the days following the parents' evening.

The parents' evening project was planned using the model proposed in Ainscow, Bond, Gardner and Tweedle, 1978.

The results showed:

a)   Parents of the able, well-attending children were most likely to attend parents' evening, whilst those of remedial, poor-attending children were least likely to attend. Though this is not proved to be causal, improving home-school contact may improve pupil attendance.

b)   However, some of the largest increases in parental attendance at parents' evenings between the January 1978 and July 1978 evenings were for the pupils in the remedial classes - between a five and tenfold increase.

Therefore, contact with such parents can be improved.

I should have gone further to see whether the

attendance of pupils whose parents started attending parents' evenings improved their child's subsequent attendance, but I did not, through lack of time.

I also did not check to see whether subsequent parents' evenings were run on similar lines and whether these had the same results. I could have asked whether the changes were lasting, but I didn't. Bear in mind at this time I made up a team of two psychologists covering nearly 90 schools, so time was at a premium. I could not see to all the casework and maintain too many research projects.

The data collected from this parents' involvement project were analysed from the aspect of disadvantaged parents.

CHAPTER SEVEN

Disadvantaged parents and contact with secondary school
(Gregory, 1980b)

Using the free meals register as an indicator of social disadvantage, it was found that:

a) Disadvantaged parents were less likely than non-disadvantaged to attend the parents' evenings.

b) The daytime visiting brought in extra parents; an extra 22% of disadvantaged parents and an extra 8% of non-disadvantaged parents.

This showed that the disadvantaged parents made greater use of the daytime facility. Care should be taken to make home-school contact arrangements that suit the parents. If they do not attend, the school must examine its arrangements, i.e. more school self-evaluation.

Some years later, in December 1984, the third author of Chapter Six being head of another secondary school by then, contacted me to get copies of the papers described in this book, in order to try and mount similar work in his present school. This is an unanticipated positive side-effect of the original research, occurring years later.

CHAPTER EIGHT

Corrective reading programme. The use of educational technology in a secondary school (Gregory, Hackney and Gregory, 1981)

CHAPTER NINE

Correct reading programme: an evaluation (Gregory, Hackney and Gregory, 1982)

In February 1979, I came across an article by Becker (1977), describing the research findings demonstrating the effectiveness of DISTAR educational programmes. These are programmes designed by Oregon University to help socially disadvantaged American children between the ages of 5-9 years, catch up academically in school. Soon after, I discovered that Corrective Reading, a programme for remedial secondary-age pupils, had also been written using the Direct Instructional model, by the authors of DISTAR. (Incidentally, DISTAR stands for Direct Instructional System for Teaching and Remediation.)

I contacted Science Research Associates (SRA), who market these programmes in the USA and Britain, to find out in which schools I might see these programmes in operation. South Tyneside was suggested.

A visit to this LEA was arranged by South Tyneside Remedial Teaching Service and took place in September 1979. The enthusiasm of the teachers using DISTAR and Corrective Reading was enormous. (At that time there were nearly 50 schools using DISTAR programmes. In May 1986, because of educational cutbacks, there were only a few schools still using the programmes. There is a continuing cycle of change.)

It was soon after this that I was again in contact with the headteacher of the study-school and mentioned the effectiveness of the Corrective Reading Programme. He was impressed and asked me to speak to the new head of the remedial department. (Good fortune and chance play a big part in action-research and innovation. It was at this point the head of the remedial department left, and the new man was very keen indeed to mount an experiment using the materials.)

Later, I learnt that the headteacher had talked to the

remedial adviser and he had agreed to pay for the Corrective Reading materials if I would send him a copy of the results. This was agreed. The evaluation models of Stufflebeam et al. (1971) and Ainscow, Bond, Gardner and Tweddle (1978) were used to plan, implement and evaluate this work.

The papers, Gregory, Hackney and Gregory (1981 and 1982) describe the results of changing the remedial curriculum. There were two groups - the experimental group received Corrective Reading and the control group received the school's current remedial provision. In January 1980, just before the experiment started, a representative from SRA came to the school and demonstrated the programme, using the experimental group of children, in front of the head, deputy head, head of remedial departments, head of English department and myself. Again, this was impressive and helped maintain the motivation for the project.

Derthick (1972) makes the connection between the flexible implementation of an innovative programme and its survival. More by chance than insightful judgement, we were flexible in the implementation of Corrective Reading. For example there was not time to teach the language comprehension component of the programme; the teaching was not scheduled every day as it should have been and there were shortcomings in the experimental design, i.e. all the experimental group came from one class and the comparison group from another. Had there been inflexibility over these problems the survival of the project might have been jeopardised. Gross et al. (1971) note that inflexible and rigid school timetables can be a special problem.

In June 1980, post-test measures were taken and the project's first year written up.

The experimental group not only showed nearly ten times better increase in reading gains, but maintained good behaviour and school attendance significantly better than the control group. This demonstrated that curriculum content and the teacher's pupil-management could cause improved attendance and good behaviour. Part of school-attendance problems are caused by the schools themselves. Again much more school self-evaluation is needed to isolate and solve school problems.

A review of the literature on the effectiveness of various educational innovations by Hoyle (1969) shows that the commitment (or otherwise) of the individual teacher to a particular teaching method is as important as the method itself. Only in hindsight have I realised that in this project the enthusiasm and commitment of the head of the remedial department for Corrective Reading was enormous and may explain the difference between our results and the lack of treatment effect in Lewis's (1982) study using Corrective Reading.

Rewarding to the authors was the finding of a review of the paper Gregory, Hackney and Gregory (1982) as far afield as the Association for Direct Instruction News, 1983, Vol. 2, No. 3, p. 3, a publication dedicated mostly to reporting Direct Instructional research from Oregon University, U.S.A. However, we have not specifically searched the science citation index which some authors do, but we have had requests for reprints from the University of Birmingham, London, a college in Worcester, Humberside School Psychological Service, two Walsall teachers, three universities in the Netherlands, Utkal University in India, a Child Guidance Centre in Nebraska, U.S.A., and two from Canadian universities.

In September 1980, the second year of the project started with more groups of children taking part. Because one group of remedial pupils was so keen, and there being no school-time available to teach them, the head of the remedial department taught them in his own time after school. A tutor on the Birmingham University Educational Psychology Training Course came to video a lesson in progress and numerous other visitors came to do likewise. This acclaim I think was very rewarding to the teachers and to the school. They had inadvertently become a 'centre of excellence' and news of this innovation was spreading by word of mouth. This is an example of the social interaction model of the spread of innovation described by Morrish (1976).

However, on a periodic visit I made to observe the teaching I found that a teacher new to the project was suffering some behaviour problems from pupils during Corrective Reading lessons. This teacher, who had a hearing loss, had had difficulties of this type in the rest of the school, was passed onto the remedial department to take smaller groups. It was apparent that he needed much more training in the use of the Corrective Reading Programme but neither the head of the remedial department nor myself had the time to do this.

However, by July 1981 the head of the remedial department felt very comfortable teaching Corrective

Reading. He said it became easier to teach, he wasn't bored with it; on the contrary, he felt secure in the knowledge that his lessons were already prepared and satisfaction in that his pupils, many of whom had not succeeded in reading for years, were making progress. However, it had been a hard second year. One group was of 16 pupils and with there being some pupils with problem behaviour this size was too large. To combat the problem, points earned during the lesson were exchanged for packets of crisps.

The third phase started in September 1981. Another weak teacher struggling in the main school was passsed to the remedial department. In March 1982 the maths department of the school was becoming interested in the sister programme, Corrective Mathematics. At this time the girls' secondary school, the subject of work in Gregory (1979) Chapter 1, became interested in using Corrective Reading with their remedial pupils. Staff came to see demonstrations of the programme and to talk with the head of the remedial department at the study school about setting it up in their school.

Noticeable was the problem of new staff being assigned to the remedial department to teach Corrective Reading. Competent teachers soon picked it up after observing a few lessons, but teachers who had problems teaching other classes in the main school continued to have problems when trying to teach Corrective Reading to smaller groups. There was not the time in the school system or the school psychological service to train such teachers.

The fourth year of the programme started in September 1982, and the head of remedial department was still saying he enjoyed teaching the programme. However, at the beginning of the fifth year in September 1983, the school merged with a neighbouring mixed comprehensive. All staff had to re-apply for their posts. Morale was very low in the school. A new head was appointed.

At this time, the head of remedial department felt he had a reputation in the city for being innovative, but was aware that inspectors were still supportive of a more child-centred approach that believed remedial children couldn't make much progress in reading and therefore it should be de-emphasised, not worked on intensively as happened with Corrective Reading. The teacher felt ill-rewarded for all his efforts by the inspectorates' attitudes. However, children in the project were now going on to do CSE subjects, a situation unheard of previously. The English department, after being cool towards Corrective Reading, was very supportive of it at this time, because it saw its department having fewer problems with poor readers.

The head of the remedial department in the merger of the two schools and the upheaval of all that implies, lost the encouragement of teachers working in the department, who probably acted as his support system. These teachers, though weak in their teaching, were serving a purpose. However, they and the headteacher who probably served a similar role, left the school. These people were replaced by a new head and a new remedial teacher. The latter was established in her way of working and was critical of Corrective Reading. At this time, the head of the remedial department suffered from exhaustion and depression, due to overwork and over-enthusiasm for his school work (he was heavily involved in the school's musical productions), family illness, the low morale in the school following the merger, and the negative attitude of the inspectors. Thus, with the lack of enough staff to teach the programme to small groups, he decided to run down the teaching of Corrective Reading. He felt that he had little energy any more. (Prescott and Hoyle (1976) talk of teachers suffering innovation fatigue.) By 1986 he had recovered his health, but the school was due for another merger with the neighbouring girls' comprehensive, where he had trained their head of remedial department in the use of Corrective Reading and with whom he was now in competition for a job in the newly merged school; a cruel irony. (Permission to recount these events and views was given by this teacher.) In November 1986 I also heard that staff committed to Corrective Reading left the girls' comprehensive and started it up in another newly merged comprehensive. This is an example of knowledge spreading from school to school by social interaction.

One of the greatest dangers to an innovation appears to be the falling away of the innovative teacher's support group; in this case the headteacher and the other remedial teachers (Gottlieb, 1981). For the external change-agent also, support is necessary, especially in times of difficulty. If this support is not forthcoming from one's own senior staff, it is necessary to actively seek it out from like-minded colleagues. In my own case three such psychologists provided this encouragement. All three publish their work and understand the problems one encounters when trying to work innovatively.

This remedial teacher is not the only professional worker who has become exhausted and depressed following involvement in an innovative project. A teacher who worked with me on a DISTAR project with severely subnormal children had very similar personal characteristics to the above teacher; hard working, caring, enthusiastic and prone to taking on too much in school.

These experiences do raise the question of the link between innovation, innovators, stress and consequent ill health. The literature on stress and the demotivation of staff, 'burn out', working in the helping agencies (Cherniss, 1980; Mattingly, 1982; Paine, 1982; Cade, 1983; Watmough, 1983; Sharron, 1986), stress in teaching (Dunham, 1978, 1981 and 1984) and white collar jobs (Cooper, 1980), may be a related issue.

Walker et al. (1976), in Chapter 3 of their book suggest that innovation:

(a) can severely increase the workload of teachers
(b) can initially undermine confidence and competence whilst new skills are being learnt
(c) can often make teachers unpopular with colleagues. They feel threatened by the new ideas and resent the extra resources innovative teachers receive
(e) can represent a career risk for teachers particularly when the innovation embodies values which may threaten the 'establishment' (e.g. if the curriculum materials embody the assumption that remedial children can learn to read - and therefore should be taught more intensively than their reading peers - as is the case with Corrective Reading and the Direct Instructional philosophy of its authors (Becker, 1977)).

If too much is attempted at once in an innovation, Kritek (1976) points out that staff cannot maintain the furious pace to which they have committed themselves. 'After a year or two they "burn out" ' says Kritek making the connection between 'burn out' stress and innovation, something not often mentioned in the educational innovation literature.

In retrospect, the good results year by year as they accumulated in this study should have been written up and widely publicised. This didn't happen. (Hakel et al. (1982) suggest that the provision of quick feedback can help to maintain the target clients' participation and interest.)

Greater care should have been taken to stop the head of the remedial department from overloading himself with too many teaching groups in previous years. Records were kept of the pupil progress in this fifth year when fewer Corrective Reading groups were taught. A future paper will look at these to see whether there was a fall-back in the rate of progress of pupils previously taught Corrective Reading and those not taught it at all.

Also, in December 1979, I went down with pneumonia, severe post-viral fatigue syndrome and depression which had been aggravated by over-work. My particular crisis followed increasing success with publications and action-research projects. This success, and the willingness of some teachers to embark on action-research in their schools, encouraged me to start too many such activities. Over-work resulted when these demanded far more time than had hitherto been anticipated.

At the same time as the Corrective Reading project, I started two others using DISTAR. I went on to have ten projects in schools and maintained them year in year out.

Eventually, it was just too much to do with all the other casework. When the 1981 Act came into operation in April 1983, under the pressure of casework and ill-health I decided to terminate maintenance of eight of my projects. For such work to continue requires the support and interest of one's senior colleagues.

CHAPTER TEN

The effectiveness of home-visits by an education welfare officer (Gregory, Allebon and Gregory, 1984)

As said earlier, this project came about from contact with the area EWO in November 1977. This led to meeting the particular EWO for this school. He was concerned about the style of work he felt under pressure to do. He was given, each week, at the school the absence slips of approximately 120 children whose absences had come to the notice of the senior master whose job it was to check attendances.

The EWO would sift these referrrals and take 80 on which to carry out home visits during that week. However, he felt that he was wasting time visiting children who were probably off school for legitimate reasons, instead of visiting far fewer but more problematic cases. When it was suggested we examine the effectiveness of his work, he was very pleased, because he felt his time could be better spent. An experimental design was drawn up for the research with very helpful advice being given by the then Chief Psychologist, Geoffrey Herbert. The project was carried out in February 1978, but not written up until a few years later. Again, this was a mistake because the optimal timing of suggestions for change would have long passed. In consequence, the project falls short of strictly qualifying to be called action-research.

The project did highlight problems with the system of coping with absenteeism in this school. The EWO, the school counsellor and the senior master all had an involvement with attendance problems, but only the EWO and senior master actually met. Roles, role relationships and communication were the problem here. What was needed was a type of innovation Dalin (1973) calls 'roles and role relationship innovation'. However, unfortunately there was not enough time to suggest changes and monitor their effect, as well as carry out the present study.

Once this project was written up, senior staff of the Educational Welfare Service had doubts about allowing it to be published. They felt that the paper and the negative results gave an unfair reflection on their service, since only one EWO was involved and it did not mention the changing practice in the service at that time. Also, they said that the EWO involved did not want publication. However, they made a request for further such research to be carried out.

A senior colleague in the Psychological Service became involved and persuaded them that there would be no incentive to do further research, if this project was not allowed to be published. They changed their minds but stipulated that the name of the EWO involved be removed from the paper. Sadly, this was done and publication went ahead.

However, some years later, in June 1985, in a chance meeting, I was able to talk with the EWO whose work was involved in the project and he gave me permission to relate his story. He said that when the question of publication arose he agreed it should be published but was pressured by senior staff to refuse publication in line with their attitudes. This he eventually did.

However, he felt involvement in the project had marked him out. He was of the 'old school' and disliked taking school non-attendance cases to court, but really wanted to work more intensively on fewer cases. He felt that his work was under scrutiny and generally under pressure. This gave rise to a prolonged illness. He was off work for 19 weeks with depression. He then took early retirement. Now in a different part-time job, he is very happy.

It is possible that in undertaking this research this EWO did draw attention to himself and his style of work, resulting in his feeling scrutinised.

This episode illustrates the need for explicit agreement for publication to be given by senior staff of a department at the outset and the need to consider the effect of possible negative consequences of the research for the future career of those involved. This is more evidence for the point about an innovation representing a career risk for those involved, made by Walker et al. (1976).

Another member of staff on seeing this research, commented that he had many ideas for research projects concerning school attendance, court appearance of poor-attending children, prosecution of cases and the work of EWOs, but felt he was not encouraged to do such work by his superiors, because the research may be politically sensitive.

Anyone leading an innovation, obviously has a responsibility to avoid allowing those he works with, (a) to take on more work in their enthusiasm than they can cope with and (b) to suffer a backlash if the results of the research are not what senior staff expected or welcome.

A principle frequently exemplified by the studies in this book is the importance of evaluating the status quo in a school situation before change is instituted, because one may inadvertently change to a worse situation or at least not ameliorate it. Such investigation and data collection acts like a 'pre test measure' and provides something with which to make later comparisons. The first, second and third studies do this. Before the parents' evening studies, evidence of the parental attendances had already been collected for past years. Before the Corrective Reading study, data on the progress of remedial pupils in past years already existed. And the tenth paper embarked on evaluating the EWO's work before any change was suggested.

It appears that it is the norm rather than the exception that innovative practices come into being, flourish for a time but then disappear. It can be the case that published papers about an innovative project are the only evidence that the innovative activities ever took place.

Having publication of a project-report in mind from the

outset can not only maintain the motivation of the staff involved but also push up the quality of the work. It is important, however, that the report writing stage should come as soon as possible after the phase of the research has come to an end. This is necessary if the report is to act as a reinforcer and as feedback to shape the next phase of the project. If nothing else a published paper publicises the project to other teachers and researchers.

Consequently it was heartening to receive requests for off-prints of this EWO research. These have come from students and academics in Bristol, Brighton, Leicester, Chichester and as far afield as Kentucky University, U.S.A., and the University of the West Indies.

This chapter has provided the background information about the processes involved in grass roots innovation. The projects are each described in more detail in the chapters.

REFERENCES

Ainscow, M., Bond, J., Gardner, J. and Tweddle, D.A. (1978) 'The development of a three part evaluation, procedure for inset courses'. British Journal of In-service Education, 4, 3, 184-90

Association for Direct Instruction (ADI News, PO Box 10252, Eugene, Oregon 97440, USA)

Baker, P. (1985) Practical Self-Evaluation for Teachers. York: Longman

Becker, W.C. (1977) 'Teaching reading and language to the disadvantaged - what we have learned from field research'. Harvard Education Review, 47, 518-43

Beishon, J. and Peters, G. (1976) Systems Behaviour. London: Published for Open University Press by Harper Row

Bowen, R.B., Green, L.L.J. and Pols, R. (1975) 'The Ford Teaching Project - the teacher as researcher'. British Journal of In-service Education, 2, 1, 35-41

Burden, R. (1978) 'Schools' systems analysis: a project centred approach.' In B. Gillam (ed.), Reconstructing Educational Psychology. London: Croom Helm

Burden, R. (1981) 'The educational psychologist as instigator and agent of change in schools: some guidelines for successful practice'. In I. McPherson and A. Sutton (eds), Reconstructing Psychological Practice. London: Croom Helm

Cade, B. (1983) 'Burnout-snuffed out fire within'. Social Work Today, 14, 18, 8-10 (11 January)

Campbell, D.T. (1969) 'Reforms as experiments.' American Psychologist, 24, 409-29

Campbell, D.T. and Stanley, J.C. (1963) 'Experimental and quasi experimental designs for research on teaching'. In N.L. Gage (ed.), Handbook of Research on Teaching. Chicago: Rand McNally

Carroll, H.C.M. (1977) Absenteeism in South Wales. Studies of pupils, their homes and their secondary schools. Swansea: University of Swansea, Faculty of Education

Cherniss, C. (1980) Staff Burnout. Job Stress in Human Services. London: Sage

Cook, T.D. and Campbell, D.T. (1979) Quasi-Experimentation. Design and Analysis Issues for Field Settings. Boston: Houghton Mifflin

Cooper, C.L. (1980) 'Work stress in white and blue-collar jobs'. Bulletin of the British Psychological Society, 33, 49-51

Dalin, P. (1973) Case Studies of Educational Innovation IV Strategies for Innovation in Education. Centre for Educational Research and Innovation (CERI). Paris: Organisation for Economic Co-operation and Development (OECD)

Dalin, P. and Rust, V.D. (1983) Can Schools Learn? Windsor: NFER - Nelson

Davie, R., Phillips, D. and Callely, E. (1985) Change in Secondary Schools. Cardiff: Department of Education, University of Cardiff. Welsh Office

Derthick, M. (1972) New Towns In-Town. Washington, D.C.: The Urban Institute

Dunham, J. (1978) 'Change and stress in the head of department's role'. Educational Research, 21, 44-7

Dunham, J. (1981) 'Disruptive pupils and teacher stress'. Educational Research, 23, 205-13

Dunham, J. (1984) Stress in Teaching. London: Croom Helm

Gottlieb, B.H. (1981) Social Networks and Social Support. London: Sage

Gregory, R.P. (1979) 'Using a social disadvantage index in a secondary school'. Remedial Education, 14, 1, 5-11

Gregory, R.P. (1980a) 'Truancy: A plan for school-based action-research'. Journal of the Association of Educational Psychologists, 5, 3, 30-4

Gregory, R.P. (1980b) 'Disadvantaged parents and contact with secondary school'. Therapeutic Education, 8, 23-6

Gregory, R.P. (1981) 'Parents' evenings in a comprehensive school. What are they for?' Comprehensive Education, 42, 24-5

Gregory, R.P. (1982) 'Attendance, social disadvantage, remedial reading and school organisation. A comparison of two neighbouring comprehensive schools'. Journal of the Association of Educational Psychologists, 5, 10, 56-60

Gregory, R.P. (1983) 'Examining a secondary school's withdrawal system of help for pupils with remedial problems. An example of within-school evaluation'. Journal of Applied Educational Studies, 12, 1, 44-5

Gregory, R.P., Allebon, J. and Gregory, N.M. (1984) 'The effectiveness of home-visits by an education welfare officer in treating school attendance problems'. Research in Education, 32, 51-65

Gregory, R.P., Hackney, C. and Gregory, N.M. (1981) 'Corrective Reading Programme. The use of educational technology in a secondary school'. School Psychology International, 2, 2, 21-5

Gregory, R.P., Hackney, C. and Gregory, N.M. (1982) 'Corrective Reading Programme: An evaluation'. British Journal of Educational Psychology, 53, 33-50

Gregory, R.P., Meredith, P.T. and Woodward, A.J. (1982) 'Parental involvement in secondary schools'. Journal of the Association of Educational Psychologists, 5, 8, 54-60

Gross, N., Giacquinta, J.B. and Berstein, M. (1971) Implementing Organisational Innovation: A Sociological Analysis of Planned Change. New York: Harper Row

Hakel, M.D., Sorcher, M., Beer, M. and Moses, J.L. (1982) Making it Happen. Designing Research with Implementation in Mind. London: Sage

Halsey, A. (1972) 'EPA action-research'. In Educational Priority Vol. 1: EPA Problems and Policies. London: HMSO

Herbert, G.W. (1976) 'Social problems: identification and action'. In K. Wedell and E.C. Raybould (eds), The Early Identification of Educationally 'at risk' Children. Birmingham: Occasional Publications number six, Educational Review, Faculty of Education, University of Birmingham

Hoyle, E. (1969) 'How does curriculum change? (2) Systems and Strategies'. Journal of Curriculum Studies, 1, 2, 230-9

Kari, J., Remes, P. and Vaahana, J. (1980) 'Disturbance and disturbers: school discipline in the light of research'. Institute of Educational Research Bulletin. University of Jyvaskyla, Finland

Katz, D. and Kahn, R.L. (1978) The Social Psychology of Organisations. Chichester: Wiley

Kritek, W.J. (1976) 'Lessons from the literature on implementation'. Educational Administration Quarterly, 12, 3, 86-102

Lewis, A. (1982) 'An experimental evaluation of a Direct Instruction programme (Corrective Reading) with remedial readers in a comprehensive school'. Educational Psychology, 2, 2, 121-35

Luthans, F. and Kreitner, R. (1975) Organisational Behaviour Modification. Brighton: Scott Foresman

Macdonald, B. and Rudduck, J. (1971) 'Curriculum research and development projects: Barriers to success'. British Journal of Educational Psychology, 41, 2, 148-54

Margulies, N. and Wallace, J. (1973) Organisational Change Techniques and Applications. Brighton: Scott Foresman

Mattingly, M.A. (1982) 'Occupational stress in group care personnel'. In F. Ainsworth and L.C. Fulcher, Group Care for Children. Concepts and Issues. London: Tavistock Publications

Miles, M.B. (1964) 'On temporary systems'. In M.B. Miles (ed.), Innovation in Education. New York: Teachers College Press, Columbia University

Miles, M.B. (1965) 'Planned change and organisation health: Figure and ground'. In R.O. Carlson et al., Change Processes in the Public Schools. Eugene, Oregon: University of Oregon

Morris, L.L. and Fitz-Gibbon, C.T. (1978) Evaluator's Handbook Program Evaluation Kit. Sage: London

Morrish, I. (1976) Aspects of Educational Change. London: George Allen and Unwin

Musgrove, F. (1971) Patterns of Power and Authority in English Education. London: Methuen

Nicholls, A. (1983) Managing Educational Innovation. London: George Allen and Unwin

Nixon, J. (1981) A Teachers' Guide to Action-Research. London: Grant McIntyre

Nuttall, D. (1986) School Self-Evaluation: Accountability with a Human Face. York: Longman

Paine, W.S. (1982) Job Stress and Burnout. Research, Theory and Intervention Respectives. London: Sage

Pasternicki, J.G. (1983) 'A study involving use of social disadvantage index'. Remedial Education, 18, 137-40

Prescott, W. and Hoyle, E. (1976) Innovation: Problems and Possibilities Curriculum Design and Development. Unit 22 and 23. Milton Keynes: Open University Press

Raia, A.P. (1974) Managing by Objectives. Brighton: Scott Foresman

Reynolds, D. (1976) 'The delinquent school'. In M. Hammersley and P. Wood (eds), The Process of Schooling. London: Routledge, Kegan Paul

Reynolds, D. (1985) Study School Effectiveness. London: Falmer Press

Robinson, P.W. and Foster, D.F. (1979) Experimental Psychology. A small N approach. A comparative analysis of large N and small N experimentation. London: Harper Row

Rutter, M., Maugham, B., Mortimore, P. and Ouston, J. (1979) Fifteen Thousand Hours Secondary Schools and their effects on children. London: Open Books

Sharron, H. (1986) 'Burnout threat to psychologists'. Times Educational Supplement, 7 February

Steel, D. (1985) 'Disruptive pupils, disruptive schools. Which is the chicken? Which is the egg?' Educational Research, 27, 1, 3-8

Stenhouse, L. (1976) An Introduction to Curriculum Research and Development. London: Heinemann

Stufflebeam, D.I., Foley, W.J., Gephart, W.J., Guba, E.G., Hammond, R.I., Merriman, O.H. and Provus, M.M. (1971) Educational Evaluation and Decision Making. Itasca, Ill: Peacock

Walker, R., Macdonald, B., Elliott, J. and Adelman, C. (1976) Innovation the School and the Teacher (1). Educational Studies. Curriculum Design and Development. Unit 27 and 28. Milton Keynes: Open University Press

Watmough, M. (1983) 'Psychologists under stress'. Journal of the Association of Educational Psychologists, 6, 2, 3-7

CONCLUSION

After completing a set of studies like the ones described, it is possible in hindsight to draw some conclusions about the problems and possibilities in carrying out such work.

1. In my experience there is no shortage of opportunities to do action-research with willing teachers and schools.

2. Setting up too many projects in too many schools is to be avoided. Inevitably, they cost more time to carry out than first anticipated. Select one target school and make it a 'centre of excellence' for the operation of a particular practice. Estimate the time span of the project in years not months. If the project is relevant to other schools, news of the activity will spread by word of mouth, and other potential targets for the innovation will present themselves.

3. Contact with the staff of the school involved in these studies came from casework referrals to the school psychological service. This contact led to the initial research projects and then these led to further developments. It was personal contact with the head, deputy head and staff that constituted the preparatory phase in this work. This served to develop a dialogue, trust and respect on both sides.

4. It is important to evaluate the status quo before introducing change.

5. Having a model of action-research that guides the activity appears essential.

6. As an external change-agent, be ready to capitalise on opportunities, often arising by chance, for action-research with teachers voicing a concern and the desire to do something about it. The research in this book

largely centred on problems already worrying senior staff of the school. Such research is likely to be the most fruitful.

7. Draw up a flexible plan and experimental design for carrying out the action-research. Be prepared to amend it in the light of changing circumstances.

8. Agree, at the outset of the project, with the appropriate people about attempting to publish the work.

9. At the planning and later stages of the project, be cognisant of the existing workload of the teachers involved. Avoid overloading them.

10. Innovative teachers need a support group in their school. Having two or three teachers involved can often provide this support. The external change-agent also needs support. He should seek out colleagues who can provide this.

11. There is a connection between innovation, stress and ill health; caution is required.

12. Beware of the possible effect a proposed project could have on the careers of the participants.

13. Allow time for writing up the research and feeding back the results and conclusions to staff at the most appropriate time. Too long a delay can mean the optimal time can have passed.

14. School self-evaluation of the type carried out in these studies can be used successfully to isolate and solve school problems. However, it is probably true to say, that those involved have to believe fervently that problem situations in schools can be changed for the better. If they doubt then a self-fulfilling prophecy will occur.

15. Apart from the project evaluating Corrective Reading which involved the purchase of materials, these projects have cost nothing in terms of funding. In all cases they have been motivated by a desire for the better utilisation of existing resources.

The cry 'we cannot do anything because we lack the resources' can be a defeatist excuse to do nothing. It is the comfortable option.

More local education authorities (LEA), support service teachers, psychologists, advisers, education college and department lecturers should as external change-agents become involved in action-research in an equal partnership with teachers in schools.

The literature on innovation is probably more easily understood and appreciated by people who have some experience of innovation in practice. The reader, new to innovating, should not be afraid to re-read this book after attempting to innovate. New insights into the problems and issues will emerge.

The staff at the study school are to be commended for having the courage and energy to take part in these studies and to carry out action-research in a way that many schools do not.

It is hoped that this book will have encouraged readers to feel more confident in critically questioning and researching problems and practices in their own school, or schools, with which they have a working relationship.

INDEX